THINKING
FOR A
CHANGE

by Michael J. Gelb and Tony Buzan

Lessons from the Art of Juggling
*How to Achieve Your Full Potential in Business,
Learning, and Life*

THINKING

FOR A

CHANGE

*Discovering the Power
to Create, Communicate,
and Lead*

Michael J. Gelb

Harmony Books • *New York*

To the memory and living legacy of
John Godolphin Bennett

Logo used on front cover is copyright of High Performance Learning.

Mind Maps is a registered trademark of the Buzan Organization.

High Performance Learning and Black Belt Business are registered trademarks of
Michael J. Gelb.

Published by Harmony Books, a division of
Crown Publishers, Inc., 201 East 50th Street, New York, New York 10022
Member of the Crown Publishing Group.

Random House, Inc. New York, Toronto, London, Sydney, Auckland

Harmony and colophon are trademarks of Crown Publishers, Inc.

Printed in the United States of America

Designed by Debbie Glasserman

Illustrated by Nusa Maal Gelb

Library of Congress Cataloging-in-Publication Data
Gelb, Michael.
Thinking for a change : discovering the power to create,
communicate, and lead / Michael J. Gelb.—1st ed.
Includes index and bibliographical references.
1. Leadership. 2. Creative thinking. 3. Human information processing. I. Title.
HD57.7.G45   1996
658.4'092—dc20   95-34495
CIP

ISBN: 0-517-59824-8

10 9 8 7 6 5 4 3 2 1

First Edition

Contents

Acknowledgments

The ideas and methods of *Thinking for a Change* have been practiced, tested, and refined in the real world by creative champions of positive change in organizations internationally. I am grateful to all who have supported this work and particularly thank: Delano Lewis, Jim D'Agostino, Marv Damsma, Ed Bassett, Bob Dahut, Dr. Madhu Jayawant, Doug Durand, Gerry Kuttas, Linda Schultz, Jim Macarthur, Joanne Lesko, Dr. Tom Jenkins, Sven and Christer Salen, Chris Morris, Pierre Carlo Falloti, Joseph Rende, and Bob Caldwell.

Very special thanks to the modern Medici, their Serene Highnesses Reigning Prince Hans-Adam II, Prince Phillipp, and Princess Isabelle Von Und Zu Liechtenstein.

In addition, I am grateful to the following people: my brilliant agent Muriel Nellis and her staff—Jane Roberts and Karen Gerwin; Connie Zwieg for introducing me to Muriel; Charlene Smith and Kristen Berry for running my office smoothly and allowing me to concentrate on writing; Peter Guzzardi for his perspicacity in recognizing the importance of synvergent thinking; Shaye Areheart, my editor at Harmony Books and her assistant, Heather Julius, for their feedback, support and enthusiasm. Cathy Raines, Dr. Marvin Hyett, Lana Israel, Dr. Barbara Bird, and Dr. Rudy Bauer for thoughtful critiques of the manuscript. Vanda North for her unceasing efforts to promote mental literacy.

Extra special thanks to: Tony Buzan—this book is a tribute to your genius, energy, and friendship; and, Nusa Maal Gelb, for your beautiful illustrations, creative collaboration, and for the greatest gift I've ever known—your love.

Preface

When I was twelve years old, I was very short. One Friday night, during services at the small synagogue to which my family belonged, the congregation stood to recite the Sh'ma, Judaism's most sacred prayer. To my extreme discomfort, I found myself at eye level with the forearm of Mr. Shaffer and—three inches from my face—numbers from a concentration camp burned into his flesh.

Shivering, I looked up at his face. His eyes seemed to radiate a lightness and gentleness. A survivor of hell, he embodied heaven.

Like many postwar children, especially those of Jewish heritage, I grew up haunted by the Holocaust. How could such a monstrosity happen? Can it be prevented from occurring again? How could life have meaning in its shadow?

Two years later, I came upon Viktor Frankl's *Man's Search for Meaning*. Frankl, an Austrian psychiatrist, was imprisoned in a concentration camp, where he and his fellow inmates lived under the most degrading conditions imaginable. Almost miraculously, Frankl discovered that although his captors had taken his liberty, they could not deprive him of his inner freedom. He created a system of psychotherapy called logotherapy, based on organizing one's life around this inner freedom.

Frankl's work gave me hope and inspiration. It launched me on a quest to understand the dynamics of the mind and spirit.

By the time I entered high school, protests against the Vietnam War were reaching their peak, and issues of racial divisiveness exploded. I remember the scent of tear gas in our school hallways after the police came to quell a near riot. The world seemed divided into two opposing camps.

People on both sides, liberal and conservative, were rarely thinking. They often reacted to events automatically and emotionally, afterward using their intellects to defend their positions. It occurred to me that the solution to many of the world's problems might lie in better understanding the nature of the human mind and in discovering how to see the world in a more accurate, unconditioned, and balanced manner.

In college, I majored in psychology, but found a disturbing gap between the academic knowledge of my professors and their behavior. It was like seeing the emperor naked. One professor, who was touted as an "international expert" in the field of nonverbal communication, wrung his hands constantly and contorted his posture while lecturing. I sat in his class, thinking, *What's wrong with this picture?*

Hoping to find more authentic sources of knowledge, I looked for teachers who "walked their talk." I traveled around the world in the proverbial "quest for truth," studying with masters from a variety of traditions. I meditated, fasted, and immersed myself in the esoteric teachings of the world's great religions.

In time, I developed a painful but increasingly liberating understanding of my own conditioned, reactive habits of perceiving and thinking. Every now and then, I experienced exceptional states of perceptual clarity and spiritual harmony.

It struck me, however, that these exceptional states were dependent on exceptional circumstances. The real challenge was not to be found on the mountaintop but in the marketplace. I continued my exploration, with a new emphasis on practical application in business and professional life.

In 1975, while studying in England, I began collaborating with Tony Buzan, the creator of mind mapping. Buzan and I share a vision of a new renaissance based on an evolving understanding of how to tap the extraordinary capabilities of the human brain. In 1978, we created the Mind and Body Seminar, a five-day residential program for leaders. For the next four years we traveled the world leading this program for a wide range of groups, including a British bank, a Swedish shipping line, an African steel manufacturer, Japanese and Australian computer companies, and American multinational conglomerates. These experiences provided a wealth of insight into the fundamental challenges facing individuals and organizations internationally.

Where could I leverage these insights for the greatest good? In 1982, I returned to the U.S. and established the High Performance Learning Center in Washington, D.C., the place where I felt thinking, communication, and leadership skills were, and still are, most urgently needed.

Since then I have worked intensively with a broad spectrum of large corporations, professional and non-profit associations, government departments, and small businesses. Much of my work is devoted to long-term efforts to change organizational cultures, helping them become more flexible in the face of unprecedented changes.

These changes parallel a revolution in everything from physics, chemistry, and brain research to telecommunications, transportation, and computer science; evolutionary developments driving, and driven by, a global "paradigm shift." Much has been written describing this movement from entropic, mechanistic, dualism to a self-organizing, organic, systems-oriented worldview and its effects on societal, organizational, and individual life. Most folks are aware that the winds of change are exceeding gale force.

An academic understanding of changing models of the world isn't much help. *Thinking for a Change* is an expression of my passion to guide you beyond a theoretical understanding of new models of the world and to discover the means, verifiable in practice, for realizing your highest aspirations for yourself, your family, and your organization.

Introduction
Step into the River ...

The flow of the river is ceaseless and its water is never the same.
—Kamo no Chome, Japanese poet (1153–1216)

Twenty-five hundred years ago the Greek philosopher Heraclitus asked, "Is it possible to step in the same river twice?" Today's electric pace of change, combined with an understanding of quantum physics, leads us to wonder: Is it possible to step in the same river once?

Twenty-five years ago, psychologist and visionary Dr. Abraham Maslow warned: "Life is moving far more rapidly now than ever before . . . in the rate of growth of facts, knowledge, techniques, and inventions. We need a different kind of human being, able to live in a world which changes perpetually, who has been educated to be comfortable with change in situations in which he has had absolutely no forewarning. The society which can turn out such people will survive; societies which do not will die."

This book is a manual for those who wish to become comfortable in our perpetually changing world. To be the "different kind of human being" Maslow prescribes *we can no longer approach information-age problems with industrial-age thinking skills.* How can we acquire the necessary skills of thinking and communicating? In *Thinking for a Change* you will learn practical, brain-based strategies for meeting these challenges.

Most of what we know about the brain has been learned in the past fifteen years. This research yields insights that can unleash your potential for personal growth and high performance. The approach in these pages is based on years of experience with thousands of people in a wide variety of environments. The skills you will learn can be applied immediately to improve the quality of your life at home and at work.

Organizations Set the Tone

In a capitalist society, business sets the social tone and, ultimately, influences the values and spiritual life of the culture at large. In today's world, societal development is a function of business and organizational development. As leadership guru Warren Bennis advises: "Because the organization is the primary form of the era, it is also the primary shaper . . . we must redesign organizations in order to redesign society along more humane and functional lines."

Increasingly, businesses are redesigning themselves, recognizing that human potential is their primary sustainable competitive advantage and that leadership is the key to its realization. Leadership is a major theme of this book. A common misconception about leadership is that it is relevant only to senior-level management in organizations. But leadership is a critically important skill for us all. In everyday life—consciously or unconsciously, for better or worse—we lead others by example. As parents, friends, and colleagues, all of us are engaged in leadership.

Thinking for a Change is based on the assumption that the thinking and communication skills of leadership can, and must, be learned. And that leadership begins with personal growth. A more fulfilling life, a happier family, a healthier organization, a saner society—they all start with your thinking, your actions, and your courage.

Let's set the stage for learning these skills by taking a glimpse at the revolution in the structure and culture of organizations. Unprecedented competition forces everyone, from retailers and restaurateurs to chemical and computer companies, to strive to integrate quality products with superior customer service at a competitive price. To meet this challenge, organizations are restructuring, reengineering, and reinventing themselves at a record pace. (See illustration.)

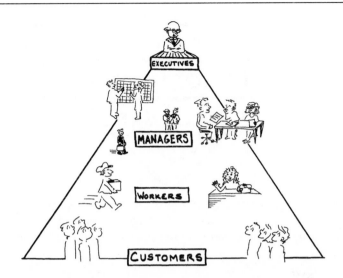

The organizational structure under which most of us were raised was bureaucratic hierarchy. In the classic pyramid, executives stood at the top, above many layers of managers. Beneath the managers were the employees, the front line of the organization. If the customers were considered at all, they were at the bottom. This kind of structure filled the perceived need for stability and control. Communication was top down and slow.

This system worked for many years, but radical developments in communication and technology spurred dramatic change. Organizations designed primarily for stability and control were threatened with extinction. Survival demanded a fundamental shift toward a more fluid, responsive structure.

Responding to the mounting tidal wave of change, the management gurus at various corporate think tanks got together and said, "Hey, the world is turning upside down, we better change our model." So they inverted the pyramid.

In the inverted pyramid, customers come first. The organization exists to serve their changing needs and desires. "Employees" are renamed "associates," to reflect a greater sense of participation and empowerment in fulfilling the organization's mission. Layers of management are dramatically thinned. A manager's role is to support associates in their attempt to serve customers. Executives provide direction and inspiration. Communication becomes two-way, with an emphasis on the speed of response.

The inverted pyramid model represents a significant improvement over the bureaucratic hierarchy, but it is still too unwieldy and mechanistic for our complex world. So here's a new model, called the Big Amoeba.

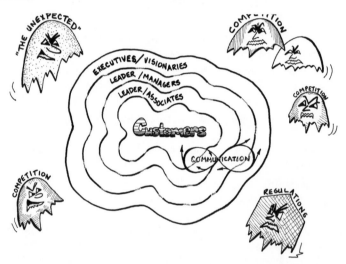

In the Big Amoeba model, the customer is at the center, surrounded by permeable membranes of leader/associates, leader/managers, and executives/visionaries. The DNA, or genetic code, of the organism is a double helix of its vision and values. Jobs, as such, no longer exist; rather, individual skill-sets are formed into mission-oriented task forces (a.k.a. "high performance teams"). As missions are accomplished, task forces are reformed. Creative thinking, judgment, and accountability are distributed throughout the organization. Communication is multidirectional, less formal, with an emphasis on team synergy.

As organizations move from unwieldy, mechanistic, hierarchical structures to more responsive, organic, and flexible forms, they become increasingly desperate to accelerate the development of their dormant human potential.

In Silicon Valley the expression "If it works, it's obsolete" has become hackneyed.

One Minute, Attila the Hun ...

Evidence for this new emphasis is everywhere. Walk into any bookstore and you'll find shelves teeming with titles on quality, customer service, empowerment, teamwork, reengineering, communication, and leadership. You might even quail at the covey of one-minute-Attila-the-Hun-swim-with-the-sharks-Zen-samurai management books!

If you work in a corporation, school, government agency, or other organization you've probably attended meetings devoted to one of the above topics. By now, you might be asking:

- How can I live a balanced life while doing quality work in less time with fewer people and a smaller budget?
- Isn't empowerment just another fad?
- If people are our most precious resource, then why has 25 percent of the workforce been fired?
- How could anyone *not* have focused on quality, service, empowerment, creativity, and leadership in the past?

Participants in these programs are understandably skeptical. They attend seminars, read memos, and go to meetings where everyone talks about quality, innovation, and teamwork. Then, if their company's stock price drops or the budget is cut, the organization becomes obsessed with cost control. Training becomes a casualty, turf wars break out, and lofty initiatives are sacrificed at the altar of short-term thinking.

Often, organizations promote cynicism by promising a "new culture" that values people and supports creativity, while key managers do nothing more than pay lip service to the "new culture" while acting according to old habits. As organizations attempt to change old habits—moving from hierarchical to more flexible structures—they run into powerful obstacles. First of all, the education that most of us received was designed to prepare us to take our place in the bureaucracy or on the assembly line. Schools paid lip service to promoting originality and independent thought while training us to be good at following rules and anticipating the requirements of authority. Moreover, individuals who grow up with, and succeed in, a hierarchical structure are understandably reluctant to give up their hard-won sense of control. Nevertheless, most people can understand the need to shift to more responsive and flexible organizational forms. This intellectual understanding, even with support from directives, training sessions, and memos from "above," is not sufficient to help people make the shift.

For the necessary changes to occur, we must look within, questioning our habits of responding to the world from a hierarchical perspective. Before we can transform organizations, we must transform ourselves.

Three Brains, Two Minds

Dr. Paul McLean, of the National Institute of Mental Health, postulates a widely accepted model of brain organization called the "triune brain." The model posits that your brain is really three brains in one. Understanding the natural organization of the brain provides a key to transforming the hierarchical mind-set.

At its base, human neural mechanisms are similar to those found in the brains of lizards or alligators. This "reptilian brain" is the source of our pecking-order behaviors as well as our tendencies toward turf definition, defense, ritualism, and stereotyped automatic reactions. According to McLean, it manifests in "slavish conformity to routine and old ways of doing things, personal day-to-day rituals and superstitious acts, obeisance to precedence as in legal and other matters, ceremonial reenactment and all manner of deception." In the words of a senior manager in an organization repeatedly lauded as "America's most admired company" by *Fortune Magazine:* "That sounds like a typical day at work."

I'm often asked to be the keynote speaker at corporate conferences usually given grand titles like "Excellence and Empowerment in the Year 2000" or "Super Quality High Performance Teams in the 21st Century!" But if these businesses were really honest, and titled their conferences based on much day-to-day behavior, the conferences would have titles such as "Cover Your Ass in the Year 2000" and "Looking Out for #1 in the 21st Century."

Of course, the reptilian brain serves as a reliable guidance system for many basic elements of survival. It is not, however, equipped to deal with a rapidly changing world.

The next level up in the triune brain model, the limbic or mammalian brain, is similar to that of a dog or a horse. This mammalian brain is the center of our emotional being. Scientists have charted the areas of the limbic brain responsible for feelings of sexual desire, anger, elation, depression, and pleasure. The limbic system also functions as the central switching station for incoming sensory data. In other words, it plays a key role in deciding what information is passed up to the most evolved segment of the brain, the cerebral cortex.

The cerebral cortex consists of the left and right hemispheres and the nerve network between them, the corpus callosum. This is the realm of consciousness, abstract thinking, planning, analysis, synthesis, and imagination. The evolution of our cerebral cortex provides what brain researcher Dr. Richard Restak describes as *"the only example in existence where a species was provided with an organ that it still has not learned how to use."*

The development of the cerebral cortex makes it possible for us to plan for the needs of others as well as ourselves. It is the seat of altruism. By creating a creature with the capacity to have concern for all living things, "nature," McLean writes, "accomplished a 180-degree turnabout from what had previously been a reptile-eat-reptile and dog-eat-dog world."

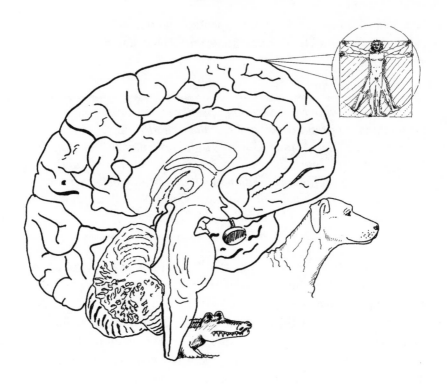

Altruism is our destiny and our salvation. Yet most attempts to live altruistically founder on the uncontrolled, unconscious reflexes of the repressed repto-mammalian self. To live a life that reflects our highest aspirations, we must acknowledge, accept, and work in harmony with our more basic nature. Carl Jung referred to this aspect of our being as the "shadow" and emphasized that by repressing, ignoring, or failing to understand it we increase its power. In his words, "Everyone carries a shadow, and the less it is embodied in the individual's conscious life . . . the denser it is. At all counts, it forms an unconscious snag, thwarting our most well-meant intentions."

As we uncover our own prejudices, pecking-order behaviors, and stereotyped, automatic reactions, our freedom of choice expands accordingly. We gain greater access to the positive side of our "instincts," improving the trustworthiness of our intuition and gut feelings.

TRIUNE BRAIN AND MASLOW'S HIERARCHY OF NEEDS	
TRIUNE BRAIN MODEL	MASLOW'S HIERARCHY
Reptilian/brain stem	**Lower level:** survival focus, food, sex, power, etc.
Mammalian/limbic system	**Middle level:** bonding, affiliation, affection, and self-esteem
Human/neocortex	**Higher level:** consciousness, altruism, big picture, long-term good of society, self-actualization

Our three brains manifest in two distinctive attitudes toward change, one dominated by atavistic, repto-mammalian tendencies, the other by our evolving consciousness. Visionary philosopher and mathematician, J. G. Bennett called these the psycho-static and psycho-kinetic, respectively.

The psycho-static mind sees change as a threat. It rejects the unknown and avoids ambiguity. This mind believes that the past determines the future, and seeks to justify its own status quo. It is motivated by fear and resists innovation, creative tension, and new ways of thinking.

Alternatively, the psycho-kinetic mind recognizes the ever-changing nature of existence, and reconciles that awareness with a sense of a changeless fundamental core. This mind embraces chaos creatively, recognizes that the present creates the future, and welcomes the unknown. It is self-reflective and seeks the truth, however uncomfortable it may be. The psycho-kinetic mind sees change as a promise.

How can we transform our fear-based, hierarchically bound, psycho-static tendencies and open ourselves to a more creative way of living? What are the practical skills of thinking and communicating for bridging the gap between talk and walk? How can we find our balance as change and ambiguity multiply?

Overview

We will begin to answer these questions in Part I of *Thinking for a Change* in which you will be introduced to a new approach to transforming hierarchical thinking. I call it synvergent thinking. **Synvergent thinking is the synergetic integration of convergent and divergent thinking modes.** Convergent thinking is focused, analytical, detailed. Divergent thinking is diffuse, multidirectional, and imaginative. People usually prefer one or the other but now we need both. As you learn the skills of synvergent thinking, you will create a new synergy of logic and imagination, reason and intuition. You will develop a talent for discerning the whole picture by integrating the big picture *and* the details. Most importantly, you will discover how to manage your life more effectively in the face of constant change and increasing complexity. A synvergent attitude leads to high performance and fulfillment, while avoiding the pitfalls of one-dimensional, have-a-nice-day positive thinking and the cynical, effete, failure formulas of sophisticated pessimists. This chapter offers a fresh look at the model of the two hemispheres of the brain and its implications for developing synvergent thinking and living a more balanced life.

In the 1980s, the American Management Association published a study concluding that the most successful managers were distinguished by their "high tolerance for ambiguity." Now, "tolerance" for ambiguity is no longer sufficient. As we approach the twenty-first century the pace of change requires that ambiguity be embraced and enjoyed.

Anyone who isn't confused doesn't really understand what is going on around here.
—scribbled in a rest room at a Fortune 500 company

Chapter 2, "Mind Mapping: The Self-Organizing Nature of Intelligence," offers a revolutionary, immediately applicable method to activate your whole brain and develop synvergent thinking. Using images, colors, and key words, mind mapping offers a more natural way to generate and organize ideas. It removes the constraints of hierarchical thinking while *improving* your ability to focus and organize. Mind mapping helps to plan everything from life goals and training sessions to presentations and dinner parties. You can use it to run more effective meetings; write reports, mission statements, and poetry; to improve your memory; and awaken creativity in all areas of life.

Chapter 3, "Problems? Synvergent Solutions!" shows you how to liberate your creative powers further by taking advantage of the natural rhythms of your mind. You will learn to allow solutions to your most important problems to "emerge" by harnessing the vast power of your subattentional consciousness. And you'll discover new strategies for integrating convergent and divergent thinking that you can apply to organizational as well as individual brainstorming.

If you apply the strategies and skills described in the first part of the book, you will be bursting with creative insights and ideas. But, without appropriate skill in communication and presentation, most ideas remain unrealized. Part II focuses on the communication skills required for managing change creatively. Much of the unnecessary angst that people suffer in chaotic times is caused by outdated, ineffective communication strategies. In most organizations, and many families, misunderstanding is pandemic and highly contagious. But there is a remedy.

Chapter 4, "Synvergent Communication," begins with an exercise that shows how your mind links ideas together. This simple exercise illuminates the most common cause of misunderstanding in everyday communication and how it can be overcome. This chapter reveals the paradox at the heart of effective communication: *We are each unique, and we are all the same in wanting to be seen and appreciated in our uniqueness.* Holding these two ideas in mind at the same time through synvergent thinking will bring a new dimension to your skills of listening and leadership. This chapter also explores the uses of mind mapping as a communication tool and some key characteristics of the finest leaders and communicators.

Chapter 5, "High Performance Presentations," shows you how to get your message across to others, how to maximize your influence through unforgettable presentations. In times of rapid change, power is up for grabs, and opportunities for advancement are won by those who can stand up and be persuasive. In the business world, presentation skill is a critical indicator of long-term success and an increasingly valuable component of leadership. Moreover, cultivating the art of presentation trains you to refine and integrate your thinking.

The final chapter, "After Enlightenment, More Laundry," offers an opportunity to integrate and organize what you have learned from this book. You will be guided to create an action plan, using your new skills for maximum personal and professional benefit.

If humanity is to pass safely through its present crisis on earth,
it will be because a majority of individuals are
now doing their own thinking.
—Buckminster Fuller

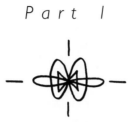

Part I

SYNVERGENT THINKING,

MIND MAPPING,

AND

PROBLEM SOLVING

Chapter 1

Synvergent Thinking

Elements of the word synvergent:

Converge: *"To tend to come together at one point"*
Diverge: *"To go in different directions from a common point"*
Verge: *"To be in the process of change or transition into something else"*
Syn: *"A prefix meaning with, together with, at the same time, by means of . . ."*
Synergy: *"Combined or cooperative action or force"*
Synergism: *"The simultaneous action of separate agencies, which, together, have greater total effect than the sum of their individual effects"*
System: *"A set or arrangement of things so related or connected as to form a unity or organic whole"*

(All definitions from the second edition of *Webster's Unabridged Dictionary*.)

In the first human societies, thinking was primarily animistic and "right brained." Native people experienced themselves as one with the earth. Every tree, every animal, every cloud possessed its own sacred spirit. Mother Earth reigned. As human societies evolved, the feeling of oneness with nature was gradually replaced by the need to control the environment. Analytical thinking began to dominate, and paternalistic societies pushed Mother Earth into the background.

Now we require a new synthesis, not a back-to-nature movement or a continuation of our shortsighted resource squandering, but rather a new integration of technology and soul, power and altruism, business and humanness. Our success and fulfillment as individuals and our continuing survival and evolution as a species, demand that we cultivate a new way of thinking—that we move beyond either/or, win/lose, us/them ways of looking at our world.

Convergent thinking is focused, analytical, detailed. It is the primary mode for balancing your checkbook, copyediting a manuscript, or pruning a tree. Divergent thinking is diffuse, free flowing, and imaginative. It is the primary mode for spontaneous humor, brainstorming, and free association. Synvergent thinking is the synergetic combination of convergent and divergent thinking. It is the primary mode for thriving with change, ambiguity, and paradox.

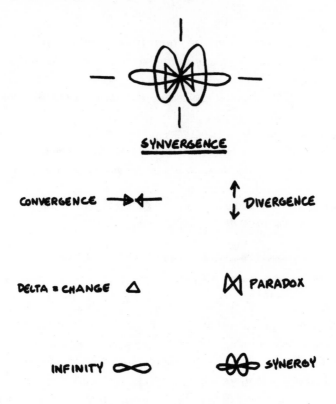

SYNVERGENCE

CONVERGENCE ⟶▶◀⟶   DIVERGENCE

DELTA = CHANGE △   PARADOX

INFINITY ∞   SYNERGY

Dancing with Dissonance

This kind of thinking has always been associated with genius. Great artists, scientists, and spiritual masters lead humanity forward by diverging from dominant paradigms, blending imaginative vision with reason and practicality. Conflict and paradox are the catalysts that propel genius to change the world. Mona Lisa's smile, Watson and Crick's discovery of the double-helix structure of DNA, and Jesus' injunction to "love thine enemy" all emerged from a transcendence of apparent opposites.

Learning to embrace change, paradox, and ambiguity is the touchstone of a creative life. Poet John Keats mused that to be creative one must demonstrate a high degree of "negative capability." He described such a person as one "capable of being in uncertainties, mysteries, doubts, without any irritable reaching after fact and reason."

The ability to embrace opposites touches the essence of being. Just as day follows night, our capacity for joy is born in sorrow. We are each the center of a unique and special universe and totally insignificant specks of cosmic dust. Of all the polarities we're challenged to reconcile, none is more daunting than life and death. The shadow of death gives life its potential for meaning. As playwright Eugene Ionesco suggests, the ephemeral often seems like the only thing of lasting value.

As change accelerates, ambiguity multiplies, and illusions of certainty become more difficult to maintain. Many people react with a kind of paralysis. They wait to be told what to think and what to do. They wait for a new job description, a new identity. The pace of change will continue to *accelerate*. Too many people are waiting and hoping for things to settle down. They won't.

Doubt is uncomfortable, certainty is ridiculous.
—*Voltaire*

As we approach the twenty-first century, the ability to dance with dissonance—to master ambiguity and paradox—can no longer be only the province of geniuses and mystics. Poise in the face of uncertainty must become part of our everyday standard of effectiveness at work and at home.

This poise requires the courage to face reality, with all its polarities and conflict. As F. Scott Fitzgerald once suggested, "The test of a first-rate intelligence is the ability to hold two opposing ideas in mind at the same time and still retain the ability to function." The synvergent thinker holds *multiple pairs* of opposing ideas in mind, simultaneously, and still functions happily.

Nobel Prize–winning physicist Niels Bohr enlightens the matter further with this complementary thought:

> There are two kinds of truth:
> small truth and great truth.
> You can recognize a small truth because
> its opposite is a falsehood.
> The opposite of a great truth
> is another great truth.

Synvergent thinkers embrace the anxiety that accompanies the search for great truths. Most people do not know when they are anxious. They react to anxiety with some form of automatic avoidance behavior such as excessive talking, reaching for a cigarette, or fantasy. To surf the tsunami of change we must learn first of all to know when we are anxious. As we become conscious of our anxiety we can learn to accept it, experience it, and free ourselves from limiting compulsions of thought and action.

To know one thing, you must know the opposite.
—Henry Moore

The willingness to make inner changes, to let go of the vestiges of old habits, anxieties, and outworn paradigms, is a prerequisite for synvergent thinking. Change management, like time management, begins with self-management. We must accept responsibility for living our priorities and managing our attitudes in the face of circumstances that are often beyond our control. To face change with equanimity, we must find something inside ourselves that is unchanging. Without this inner work, techniques and strategies of change management are shallow palliatives.

Of course, this inner work isn't easy. As Emil Sinclair pleads in Herman Hesse's *Demian,* **"All I ever wanted was to live from the**

promptings of my true self. Why was that so very difficult?" This journey demands that we shine the light of consciousness on deeply grooved habits. This demands a relentless process of questioning that leaps the pitfalls of narcissism and self-indulgence.

~~~~~~

Man must strive with all his might to become what he really is.
—*Meister Eckhart*

~~~~~~

Perhaps the greatest challenge for those who would master change is the willingness to take action in the face of uncertainty. We must be commited to act—even while aware that we could be wrong. *This commitment is easier to make when you understand that your brain is designed over millions of years of evolution to be the most profoundly powerful learning and problem-solving tool in all known creation.* Your brain is more complex, flexible, and powerful than any super-computer. Its neural circuitry is estimated to be at least 1,400 times more complex than the entire global telephone network.

As you read these words, your 30 billion neurons are shimmering with over 100,000 chemical reactions every second. The number of possible connections or patterns of thought that your brain can make is significantly greater than the number of atoms that exist in the universe. The best estimate of the number of atoms in the universe is 10^{200}. One conservative estimate of your brain's potential to make connections, offered by Prof. Pyotr Anokhin of Moscow University, is the number 1 followed by 6.5 million miles of standard-sized IBM typewritten zeros.

FEAR IS THE MIND KILLER

What becomes of this remarkable birthright? More often than not, it is compromised by fear—the fear of failure and embarrassment, passed on from generation to generation, that locks in fear of the unknown.

This pattern is often exacerbated in the first few years of school. Think back to your school days. Remember when you or someone else in your class was very excited about answering a teacher's question—"Ooh, ooh, please call on me!" Remember the enthusiasm with which you blurted out a truly original, creative, self-expressive answer? And the teacher responded, "No, that's not the answer I was looking for." Remember the mocking laughter of the rest of the class, followed by a little voice inside each child's mind, warning, "Never, ever do that again."

In most cases, schooling does not develop originality, delight in ambiguity, or self-expression. Rather, the thinking skill that's rewarded is figuring out the "right answer"—that is, the answer held by the person in authority, the teacher. This pattern holds through university and postgraduate education, especially in a class where the professor wrote the text.

Furthermore, our way of testing and grading reinforces a pernicious pattern of short-term, superficial thinking. In a study done at Harvard University, summa cum laude graduates who received all A's in their final exams were given those same exams one month after graduation. They all failed. As brain researcher Leslie Hart observes, "Final exams are final indeed."

The fear-based, authority-pleasing, rule-following approach to education may have served to provide society with assembly-line workers and bureaucrats, but it does not do much to prepare people for the world as it is today.

I Can't / I Can: Psycho-Physical, Self-fulfilling Prophecy

Growing up with a fear of failure and embarrassment builds a pattern of thinking that stifles initiative and dulls the ability to think synvergently. This "I can't" pattern is a psycho-physical, self-fulfilling prophecy that manifests in a wide variety of life areas. One classic example is the "I can't" associated with singing, which often originates in the following scenario.

It's choir day in the third grade and Johnny is singing along with the rest of the children when his teacher, Ms. Tracy, stops the class. "Someone is singing off key. Johnny, I think it is you. Come up to the front of the room and sing." Mortified, Johnny sings, and he is more off key than before. Everyone laughs.

What happens to Johnny's vocal chords under the stress of this embarrassment? They contract. What does this do to the quality of his singing voice? It gets worse. How does the response to his solo affect him? He decides, "I can't sing," and for the rest of his life he does not sing. His "I can't" becomes a self-fulfilling prophecy.

Another common "I can't" is "I can't draw, I'm not artistic": It is time for art class in the fourth grade at Clifton Elementary School and all the kids are busy drawing airplanes. David's drawing is rather abstract. When the teacher puts the drawings up on the wall at the end of class, David's is not among them. Suzy's fate is even worse. Her unconventional, idiosyncratic representation of an airplane, hung on another wall, is offered as an example of what an airplane does not look like.

Both David and Suzy decide "I can't draw, I'm not artistic." For the rest of their lives they do not even try.

Other common pessimistic, self-fulfilling prophecies include: I can't speak in public, be creative, do mathematics, dance, lose weight, make enough money, get along with the opposite sex, be happy. . . .

Organizationally, the "I can't" becomes the "we can't." I lead many seminars for junior- to senior-level managers, where the participants are very excited about what they learn but hesitant to apply it in the workplace. When asked the reason for their hesitancy, they usually say something like, "We can't apply it because 'they' won't let us."

I once encountered a heavy dose of the "they" phenomenon during interviews prior to a series of seminars for the management team of a $600 million company. Over five weeks I led mixed-level groups of up to 70 people, until all 580 managers, including the CEO and all senior executives, had attended. "They" were all there. At the beginning of each session, I asked everyone to turn to the person sitting next to him or her and write "They" on the colleague's name tag.

We are "They."

Organizationally and individually, creative things get done by people who think "I can." An "I can" attitude is grounded in a willingness to take responsibility for one's own life and acting as though thoughts and actions flow primarily from choices not circumstances. The "I can" attitude is a self-fulfilling prophecy that leads to success. It turns the vast potential of your brain "On," awakening and focusing your power to learn and create.

Half Empty and Half Full: Synvergent Optimism

Of course, it is easy to maintain a positive attitude when everything is going your way. The real test comes when things are not going well. **The greatest long-term predictor of success for individuals and organizations is resilience in the face of adversity.** Individuals and organizations who view their setbacks in the context of progress are much more likely to continue in their efforts toward success. As psychologist Karen Horney discovered, most people actually succeed when they *commit* to do whatever it is they want to do in life.

Most of what people describe as failure in their lives, Horney discovered, is a function of withholding commitment. In other words, they give up prematurely and label the experience a failure. Shakespeare understood this when he wrote, "Our doubts are traitors and make us lose the good we oft might gain by fearing to attempt."

Persistence is a critical key to success, and an "I can" attitude is the key to persistence. Dr. Martin Seligman, author of *Learned Optimism,* points out that "I can't" thinking tends to be self-fulfilling because it short-circuits persistence. Seligman's research, over more than two decades, shows that pessimists tend to give up when confronted by adversity, even when success may be right around the corner. Living under Murphy's law, they have, in his words, "the knack for snatching defeat out of the jaws of victory."

Seligman's research also demonstrates that "I can" thinkers perform better at work, school, and in athletics. Optimists regularly outperform the predictions of aptitude tests. Their resistance to colds and other illnesses is superior and they recover faster from illness and injury. And, optimists make significantly more money.

Seligman also discovered that pessimists are generally more accurate in their assessments of reality. Pessimists assume that optimists are people who do not yet have all the facts. Optimists really do seem to look at the world through rose-colored glasses. The results of Seligman's long-term studies demonstrate, nevertheless, that better results are obtained by erring on the side of optimism.

My observation and experience reveal, however, that the *most* successful individuals take a synvergent perspective: combining the pessimist's perspicacity and critical analysis with the optimist's perseverance, creativity, and "I can" attitude.

Aim to see the world as clearly as you can in a context of synvergent optimism.

You can succeed by choosing to persevere when confronted with difficult conditions and apparent failure.

You can think "I can" when those around you say you can't.

You are free to embrace a psycho-kinetic attitude—to live a life that springs from courage and love more than fear and despair.

A synvergent thinker knows that courage is not the opposite of fear, but rather the willingness to forge ahead in the face of fear. Synvergent thinkers maintain a positive course amid torrents of chaos. The "I can" attitude offers a springboard to success. But as the pace of change accelerates, uncertainty multiplies exponentially. Old, hierarchical and reactive ways of organizing the world are no longer sufficient. We must discover new skills to navigate in swirling oceans of ambiguity. Synvergent optimism is just the beginning. Let's proceed by learning more about the nature and extent of our potential and the attitudes and thinking skills that awaken it.

The Synvergent Brain:
Getting Your Head Together

One of my favorite tools for introducing people to synvergent thinking is the model of the two hemispheres of the cerebral cortex. Although information on the brain's hemispheres has received a great deal of popular attention, it is frequently misunderstood and misapplied. Let's review and update it, focusing on how to apply this understanding to improve the quality of your life at work and at home.

Prof. Roger Sperry, who won the Nobel Prize in medicine and physiology in 1982, conducted much of the original research in this field. In the early years of his work, he and his colleagues discovered that in most cases the left hemisphere of the cerebral cortex processed convergent thinking: logic, language, mathematical reasoning, attention to detail, sequence, order, and analysis. The right hemisphere seemed to process divergent thinking: rhythms, colors and shapes, daydreaming, imagination, and synthesis.

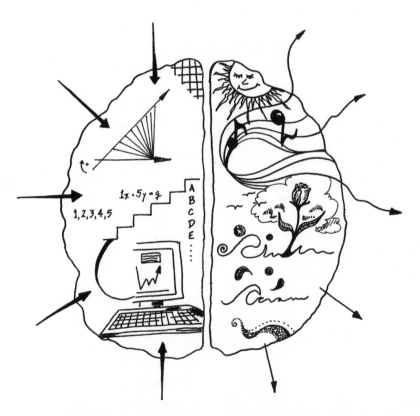

The two hemispheres of the cerebral cortex: left, convergent thinking; right, divergent thinking.

Most individuals seem to have a tendency for one of these two modes to dominate. If you're thinking, I need more evidence, where can I obtain the original research papers? How exactly did Sperry ascertain his results? you probably are left-brain dominant (see Bibliography for references). If instead you are thinking, Cool! This feels right to me, you're probably right-brain dominant.

Similarly, if you wished this book contained a test complete with checklist and scoring system so that you can better determine your dominant mode, you are probably the more analytical-type thinker. If you don't really like those sorts of things because you already know what you are, you're probably more intuitive. And if you're reading this book in page sequence, starting with page 1 and working your way in order through the text, you are probably a more sequential type.

Since the early days of Sperry's research, a tremendous amount of research has been done on the two hemispheres. It now appears that the left hemisphere is capable of performing many of the functions of the right and vice versa. Moreover, the left-right dominance dichotomy seems to hold true for only about 90 percent of right-handed people and 60 percent of left-handers. The others have either a reversed or unclear dominance pattern. Researchers also have found different brain dominance patterns in people who rely on pictographic writing, such as the Japanese.

There also are key differences between women and men. Women have a better developed corpus callosum, the network of nerve fibers that connects the hemispheres. This might explain why women often seem to be more in touch with their intuition. Researcher Justine Sergeant suggests that the left hemisphere is responsible for processing things that are smaller in the visual field, such as the tiny writing of many engineers, and that the right hemisphere is responsible for things that are larger in the visual field, such as pictures. Hence the association of the right hemisphere with artistic awareness.

An exact understanding of the two hemispheres still awaits us. Meanwhile, it is probably best to think of left brain and right brain as *metaphors* for convergent and divergent thinking, respectively. For our purposes, the important thing is that *wherever they are located and whatever our tendency in terms of dominance, our highest level of functioning is realized when we synergize these two modes.*

Modeling Genius

In the groundbreaking bestseller, *Buzan's Book of Genius,* Tony Buzan and coauthor Raymond Keene, offer, for the first time, an objective ranking system for history's 100 greatest geniuses. (Genius scale rankings will be placed after the names of the geniuses referred to in the remainder of this book.) Buzan and Keene emphasize that the greatest brains from both science and art are those who integrate logic and imagination . . . synvergent thinkers.

For example, Albert Einstein, one of the great geniuses of all time (tenth on Buzan and Keene's scale) revolutionized our understanding of the universe. His mathematical and scientific skills, as well as his employment by the Swiss government patent office, attest to the power of his logical mind. But what were Einstein's other interests? He loved music, especially the violin, as well as painting and sailing. But his most important pursuit, by his own admission, was to play imagination games. Einstein took time on a daily basis to make "thought experiments."

One day early in his career, Einstein went for a walk on a grassy hillside. He closed his eyes, enjoying the warmth of the sun and imagined that he was riding on a sunbeam out into the universe. In his mind's eye, he traveled into eternity and was shocked to discover himself returning to the place from which he began.

If you travel forever in one direction and return to the place where you began, what does that tell you about the universe? Obviously, it must be curved. As a result of this and other imagination games, Einstein intuited his theory of relativity. Of course, he also possessed the discipline, focus, and mathematical skill to translate his leap into the universe into the language of science so that others could understand it.

What about the previous revolution in our understanding of the universe, facilitated by Sir Isaac Newton (sixth all-time according to the *Book of Genius*)? He's often thought of as the ultimate logical mind, the "creator" of our orderly universe. (Can you imagine how messy the universe must have been before Newton revealed the theory of gravity—things floating everywhere?)

The old pound note in Britain portrayed Newton as a dour, pinched-faced scientist, surrounded by codes, equations, and scientific instruments. But, in addition to having a great logical mind, Newton was a dreamer: childlike, playful, innocent. Newton's *Optics,* one of his great works, was inspired when a glass broke in his cabin. Sunlight shone through his open window, striking the broken glass and creating a prism effect. A tiny rainbow appeared on his wall. Quickly, Newton collected all the glass he could find, smashed it, and wrote in his journal, "I filled my cabin with rainbows."

In describing his own process of thinking, Newton said: "I do not know what I may appear to the world, but to myself I seem . . . like a boy playing on the seashore . . . diverting himself, and then finding a smoother pebble or prettier shell than ordinary, while the greater ocean of truth lay all undiscovered before me."

Newton, who wrote more on metaphysics than physics, was a dreamer, a mystic. He was childlike, innocent, disciplined, and focused. A rigorous scientist. A balanced brain. A synvergent thinker.

August Kekule, discoverer of the structure of the benzene ring, made his breakthrough discovery while dreaming in an easy chair before his fireplace. Although there's some debate as to whether Kekule was aided by a couple of fine brandies, it is clear that he had a reverie in which he saw a snake chasing its own tail. As he later recalled, "the atoms were gamboling before my eyes . . . all twining and twisting in a snakelike motion . . . one of the snakes siezed its own tail, and the form whirled before my eyes." Kekule realized upon awakening that the atomic serpents had formed themselves into the missing molecular puzzle piece.

You can bet that unless Kekule had spent careful hours in the laboratory, he probably never would have had this dream. And without the focus, persistence, and technical skill to translate this leap of imagination into the language of science, it would have been nothing more than a meaningless fantasy. Kekule was both a dreamer and a disciplined scientist. When he spoke at the Royal Academy, accepting the honors for his great breakthrough, he concluded by saying, "We must all learn to dream."

As we explore the history of science, it becomes difficult to find an example of a breakthrough discovery or great achievement that did not result from a dream, a daydream, an accident, or a chance happening that moved the dreamer to diverge from the dominant paradigm. The great historical figures we call scientific geniuses are those who rather than ignore or dismiss the promptings of their imagination integrated them with their knowledge of scientific method.

WHAT ABOUT ARTISTS?

Study the science of art and the art of science. Learn how to see and remember that everything is connected to everything else.
—Leonardo da Vinci

What, then, of the great artists? People tend to think of painters, for example, as being "flaky," living on the fringe of the right hemisphere. If a painter had the discipline to keep a diary, skeptics think, it might read something like this: Arose 11:45 A.M. Drank three cups extra-strong espresso coffee. Smoked mind-altering substance. Sloshed paint on canvas. Mushed it around. Sold for enormous sum. Debauched for rest of day.

But when you look into the lives of many of the great painters you find a remarkable attention to detail and discipline. Great artists understand that organization and discipline set the stage for the creative act. Attention to detail and intense analysis were the hallmark of artists such as Caravaggio, Cezanne (49), Dali (37), Duchamp (72), Klee, Michelangelo (5), O'Keefe, Picasso (24), Raphael (85), Rembrandt (96), Seurat, and Titian (91). A successful artist needs a practical knowledge of optics, the psychology of perception, geometry, and chemistry. These elements turn imagination into reality.

One myth that has arisen about the information on the two hemispheres is that the right hemisphere is the province of creativity. This is wrong. Creativity is a function of the whole brain working in harmony. Without organization and logic, creativity is stillborn.

The number one genius of all time—the last person to be world master of both science and art—was Leonardo da Vinci. Leonardo championed the balance of logic and imagination, the marriage of science and art. His scientific notebooks, his studies of water flowing and human anatomy are beautiful, evocative, expressive works of art, not dry technical drawings. The plans for his paintings and sculptures are highly disciplined and detailed.

In his treatise on painting, *Trattato della Pittura,* da Vinci emphasized, for example, that the ability of the artist to effectively express the beauty of the human form is predicated on a profound study of the science of anatomy. Lacking an appreciation borne of a detailed analysis of bone structure and muscular relationships, the would-be artist was liable to draw "wooden and graceless nudes that seem rather as if you were looking at a stack of nuts than a human form, or a bundle of radishes rather than the muscles. . . ."

It's interesting to note that da Vinci also cultivated the balanced use of both sides of his body, practicing writing with both left and right hands. He was psycho-physically ambidextrous.

LEFT-BRAIN BIAS

From a very early age, we are taught to break apart problems, to fragment the world. This apparently makes complex tasks and subjects more manageable. But we pay a hidden enormous price: we can no longer see the consequences of our actions. We lose our intrinsic sense of connection to a larger whole.
—Peter Senge

Our society often pays lip service to the idea of the balanced, Renaissance individual, but in practice we suffer from a pandemic of "half-witted" thinking. Looking back to the first few years of your schooling, what were the first three subjects on which you were graded, judged, and evaluated? Probably the proverbial "3 R's": readin', 'ritin', and 'rithmetic, with an emphasis on the more analytical, sequential, convergent mode of thinking.

If you scored A's in reading, writing, and arithmetic, how were you described by parents, teachers, and peers? "Class brain." "Smart." "College material."

What if you excelled, instead, at tapping out innovative rhythms on your desk, if you loved to make colorful, multidimensional doodles while looking out the window and having great daydreams. What if you were tops in your class at making imaginative comments to your teacher? Then you probably were labeled "learning-disabled," "hyperactive," "a problem child."

Much of our schooling builds in a left-brained, "I can't" bias. In the words of Professor Sperry: "Our education system, as well as science in general, tends to neglect the nonverbal form of intellect. What it comes down to is that modern society discriminates against the right hemisphere."

Sperry wrote those words in 1973, and the phenomenon still holds true. If there is a cut in your community's education budget, what subjects tend to be eliminated? Usually art, drama, music, physical education, and foreign language. People often urge, "Let's get back to the basics." But by any measure—whether through a survey of the great brains of history or the scientific work of Sperry and his colleagues, or just plain old common sense—*the basics are the skills of logic and imagination taught in harmony.*

Similarly, in both Britain and the United States, one can witness a battle between the traditional and progressive approaches to education—the traditional being more left brained, while the progressive approach tends to err on the side of being overly "right." In reaction to the overregimentation, high failure rates, and narrowness of traditional educational approaches, progressive education often suspends discipline and encourages open classrooms while focusing on social skills development with lots of finger painting and drawing. The result: students who are expressive and in touch with their feelings, but can't read, write, or do arithmetic.

Advocates of the right brain are prone to romanticize its powers and downplay the importance of discipline, logic, and convergent thinking. They should heed the admonition of Dr. Michael Gazzaniga, a colleague of Dr. Sperry: "The left brain—don't leave home without it!"

The most effective educators understand the importance of a whole-brain approach. Every year, in most communities, a corporation or educational association sponsors some kind of teacher-of-the-year award. Local television stations often cover the event. One example that stands out began with the camera panning a class of kids dressed as seventeenth-century citizens of Salem, Massachusetts. Suddenly, their teacher came wheeling into the room on a skateboard, wearing a black robe and a witch's hat. The kids were enthralled.

A reporter interviewed the children, quizzing them on their knowledge of the Salem witch trials. The kids didn't miss a beat. They knew all the answers cold. Asked how he felt about his skateboarding teacher, one little boy said, "She is the greatest . . . our class is fun and we learn a lot." Pressed by the reporter, he added, "Yeah, she's also the strictest teacher in the school."

The most productive educational environments synergize the best of the traditional and progressive approaches. They integrate seriousness and play, art and science, discipline and fun, logic and imagination.

"THE DEATH OF COMMON SENSE"

Without the balancing influences of intuition and awareness of a larger context, left-brain thinking paralyzes intelligence and perverts common sense. Many of the frustrations of everyday life are caused by systems that attend to the parts, while missing the whole picture. I recently witnessed a classic example on a trip from Dulles airport in Washington, D.C. The euphemistically named "mobile lounge" that was transporting thirty of us to the midfield terminal broke down. Trapped inside (insurance regulations prevent the airport authority from allowing people to just get out and walk) a number of people became agitated as their flight time approached. More than one of the passengers pleaded with the driver to radio ahead to inform the airline so they could hold the flight until repairs were completed. After a delay of twenty minutes the "mobile lounge" arrived at the terminal and many of the passengers discovered that their flight had just left. They confronted the agent in charge. He responded that the message was not received. He pointed out that "the airline and the airport authority have nothing to do with one another." Indeed.

Left-brain imbalance has infected every aspect of public life. Our legal system, government agencies, and many corporations are drowning in oceans of overregulation. Obsession with order and control has become a kind of psychosis that destroys common sense and good judgment. In *The Death of Common Sense,* Philip Howard offers story after story of staggering stupidity and bureaucratic waste caused by ignoring context, interrelationship, and awareness of the big picture. Howard writes, "Rationalism, the bright dream of figuring out everything in advance and setting it forth precisely in a centralized regulatory system, has made us blind. Obsessed with certainty, we see almost nothing." He emphasizes that we must remember that "everything is interconnected" and that "judgment and balancing are always required."

THE BUSINESS BRAIN

Today, business demands that people be more creative, empowered, and adaptable, yet hiring and promotion still tends to be based largely on left-brain credentials. Ned Hermann, founder of the Whole Brain Corporation and a pioneer in encouraging "whole-brain" hiring and human-resource policies, developed a test to determine the extent to which people are left- or right-brained dominant.

In his workshops, Hermann has been known to take those who test out as "ultra left" and "ultra right," and give them a special assignment. They are allowed two hours to complete it. The ultra-left-brained group returns exactly on time, having completed a typewritten report, with all the i's dotted and t's crossed. Beautifully organized, their report is painfully boring and uninspiring. The ultra-right-brained group involves itself in a major philosophical debate on the meaning of the assignment. They return at different times with ideas scratched on scrap paper, disorganized and generally useless.

Hermann then puts the two groups together with a facilitator who guides them as they work together on another task. They return on time with a balanced, organized, creative product. The lesson of Hermann's work is obvious: it is important to create balanced brain teams.

More often than not, however, individuals tend to polarize by brain style. The left-brain dominants in the finance department gather by their coffee machine, look over at the right-brained marketing people, and say: "Those flaky dreamers have their heads in the clouds. They don't understand the bottom line like we do." Meanwhile, at the right-brained water cooler (spring water, of course), the right-brainers are eyeing the left-brainers and saying: "What tiny minds those bean counters have. They don't see the whole picture like we do."

Individuals often fall into a similar trap internally. Left-brainers think, "I'm sorry, I'm left brained. I can't possibly be creative or imaginative." And right-brainers make the mistake of programming themselves: "Well, I'm right brained, I can't possibly come to meetings on time."

To compete effectively today individuals and organizations must cultivate balance. Prof. Henry Mintzberg, of the McGill University Faculty of Management, points out that the most effective executives integrate analytical input with holistic, intuitive thinking skills. He emphasizes that successful executives are capable of "revelling in a climate of calculated chaos."

Prof. Weston Agor of the University of Texas in El Paso has studied thousands of managers in business, government, and academia. His textbook, *Intuitive Management: Integrating Left and Right Brained Skills,* also emphasizes the importance of the balanced brain. Agor suggests that the most successful organizations blend engineering with "imagineering."

After testing hundreds of managers, consultant Jacqueline Wonder, author of *Whole Brain Thinking,* found that the finest managers are able to transcend their natural brain dominance patterns, flexibly employing both modes as a situation demands. She emphasizes that the most effective leaders are able to "shift left" when writing reports or analyzing data and then "shift right" when brainstorming or counseling a subordinate.

Since 1978 I've worked with thousands of managers at all levels. Some are disciplined, analytical, serious, thorough planners, focused on substance; others are flexible, intuitive, playful, improvisers, focused on process. The very best are those who balance discipline and flexibility, analysis and intuition, seriousness and play, planning and improvisation, substance and process. Balanced brains. Synvergent thinkers.

Studies by educational psychologist and creativity expert Prof. E. P. Torrance and others demonstrate conclusively that individuals can change their imbalanced styles of thinking and learning through brief but intensive training.

LEADERS *AND* MANAGERS

In *When Giants Learn to Dance: Mastering the Challenge of Strategy, Management, and Careers in the 1990s,* Rosabeth Moss Kanter elucidates some of the common dissonant challenges faced by citizens of the organizational world:

- Think strategically and invest in the future—but keep the numbers up.
- Be entrepreneurial and take risks—but don't cost the business anything by failing.
- Continue to do everything you're currently doing even better—and spend more time communicating with employees, serving on teams, and launching new projects.
- Know every detail of your business—but delegate more responsibility to others.
- Become passionately dedicated to "visions" and fanatically committed to carrying them out—but be flexible, responsive, and able to change direction quickly.
- Speak up, be a leader, set the direction—but be participative, listen well, cooperate.
- Throw yourself wholeheartedly into the entrepreneurial game and the long hours it takes—and stay fit.
- Succeed, succeed, succeed—and raise terrific children.

I bought a humidifier and a dehumidifier, put them in the same room, turned them on, and let them fight it out.
—Steven Wright, humorist

Reconciling these contradictions is not easy. We are called to be leaders and managers, simultaneously. Before we can integrate these skills it is necessary to clarify the difference between them.

Webster's defines leadership as "the ability to show the way by going before or along; the capacity to lead." *Webster's* defines manager as "one who conducts affairs with economy and frugality; a good economist; one who is skilled in contriving, planning or intriguing so as to accomplish his purpose."

Prof. John Kotter of Harvard Business School and others have emphasized the important distinction between management and leadership. Managers focus primarily on controlling complexity, monitoring performance, guiding systems, planning budgets, and supervising the implementation of plans. In other words, the primary mode of the traditional manager is convergent, oriented toward stability.

The leader's primary focus is divergent, oriented to change. The leader is charged with framing and communicating the vision. Perhaps the most important tool of communication is the example the leader sets. Leaders assume responsibility for guiding the organization into the future.

In a recent presentation, Professor Kotter showed four videotapes made while conducting a study of the leadership/management styles of senior business executives. Kotter's graduate student assistants conducted extensive interviews with key associates of these leaders/ managers.

Frank Borman, former president of Eastern Airlines, was the subject of the first tape. It showed Borman addressing his employees. The gist of his message was that the problems the company was experiencing were the fault of the people in the audience. When Kotter's students asked Borman's associates to rate Borman as leader or manager, they replied that he was basically an astronaut.

The next videotape was an inspirational speech by Donald Burr, former chairman of People's Express Airlines. Burr, who had led People's Express to dizzying heights of success in a very short time, was incredibly charismatic. His speech was like a revival meeting. Yet, as Kotter's graduate students discovered, Burr was so involved in the vision and the culture he created at People's Express that he made a fatal error. He stopped listening to those around him who were actually managing the business. One by one, they resigned. What followed was one of the most dramatic collapses in the history of American business.

The third videotape was of Edward Hennessy, the former chairman of Allied, a giant conglomerate. Hennessy seemed the classic organization man: buttoned down, tight-lipped, uninspiring. His presentation suggested an almost Orwellian concern with numbers and statistics. Hennessy was presented as an example of the ultimate imbalanced manager, with little or no leadership ability. Through his tenure, this massive company grew at a very low rate with minimal return to stockholders. Ironically, Hennessy made a fortune from stock options when he left Allied because the stock rose so dramatically on the news of his retirement.

The last videotape was a surprise and a delight. It was a speech by Mary Kay Ashe, founder of Mary Kay Cosmetics. Although her speech had the revival-meeting quality of Burr's address, there was also a sense of a more down-to-earth perspective. One woman after another approached Mary Kay and, in deeply emotional ways, thanked her for the opportunity she had created.

Kotter then told a story about the time Mary Kay was invited to Harvard Business School. She showed up with her blond bouffant hairdo, wearing her pink dress, driving her pink Cadillac. A small entourage of associates accompanied her. Kotter recounted Mary Kay's grace in fielding students' questions. When she encountered a difficult technical question, she introduced an associate who provided a detailed, thorough, and very impressive answer that silenced any skeptics in the audience.

The graduate assistants asked Mary Kay's staff whether she was more a manager or a leader. They initially answered that she was a fantastic leader, inspirational, and that people would give their very best for her. But upon further reflection, the staff asked the graduate assistants if the fact that Mary Kay surrounds herself with great managers, and leads them effectively, qualifies her as a great manager? The graduate students replied, yes, indeed.

As these stories suggest, the key to long-term success is to integrate the skills of leadership and management. Kotter's model is an excellent tool for assessing yourself and others in terms of this balance.

Balancing leadership and management is as important at home as it is at work. As a parent, one must be both leader and manager. We must guide the "culture" of the family, creating and nurturing a vision of possibility for our children and, most important, providing an example of the vision-in-action. At the same time, of course, we must manage the household, monitor performance, and adhere to budgets.

Leaders are often compared to shepherds. A shepherd must be out front, guiding the flock in the right direction toward greener pastures.

L E A D E R S H I P

M A N A G E M E N T

The most effective individuals and organizations can be found in the upper right "Mary Kay" quadrant.

But if there's no one checking in the back, the sheep can be caught in brambles, fall into ditches, or be eaten by wolves. A manager needs to walk behind the sheep and count them, control them, monitor their progress. If we have only management, we might have our full complement of sheep, but they could wander in to the wrong pasture or even fall off a cliff. If we have only leaders, we might arrive at the right pasture, and turn around to find only three sheep behind us.

Author Stephen Covey compares the function of managers to individuals hacking their way through the jungle. The leader is the one who climbs up a tall tree and shouts, "Wrong jungle!" All too often, the response of the managers is, "Be quiet, we're making progress!"

We must find a way to be flexible enough to lead from the front *and* watch the back of the flock; to climb the tree, take the broad view, and then hop down and help cut the path.

Warren Bennis says, "Managers do things right; leaders do the right thing." To do the right things right, we must synergetically integrate convergent and divergent perspectives.

In the next chapter you will learn an immediately applicable method for developing this integration. But first, let's set the stage by exploring the practical business of developing a more balanced approach to living.

When you come to a fork in the road take it.
—Anon

Balance Your Life

Individually, educationally, and organizationally, we now require a balanced, synergetic use of our brains. This integration must become the new standard of basic competence if we are to thrive on the challenges of our time. Of course, there is a considerable gap between the theoretical understanding of the idea of the balanced brain and the actual habits of balanced living. To accelerate your own personal evolution of a more balanced brain you can:

- Take brain breaks
- Create a brain-nourishing environment
- Keep a journal or notebook
- Record your dreams
- Take time for solitude
- Appreciate others with different brain dominance
- Pursue your ideal hobby
- Practice meditation
- Develop psycho-physical fitness
- Cultivate ambidexterity
- Encourage "both sides" of your children
- Transcend sexual stereotypes

Let's explore these one at a time.

TAKE BRAIN BREAKS

Most people find the ideal of balance very attractive, but the reality eludes them because they are just "too busy." As the pace of change accelerates so does the pace of our lives. Death may be nature's ultimate way of telling you to slow down but nervous breakdowns are frequently the penultimate message. Do you know anyone who has had a nervous breakdown? If you work in an organization, chances are that you do. And there's a good chance that you'll know many more in the future. If you pay careful attention, however, you will significantly reduce your chances of becoming one of them.

The pattern that leads to the classic nervous breakdown might be described this way.

Sam was very ambitious, so he skipped breakfast and picked up a doughnut and coffee on the way to work—he got more work done that way. He was addicted to business lunches. He always took work home at the end of the day and over the weekend. He never took his full vacation, and had no time for hobbies. Just work, work, work.

Sam's career progressed nicely. Over a period of ten years, he received a few promotions and was making good money. One day, Sam came to work as usual and entered his cubicle when suddenly it was as though the right hemisphere of his brain looked over to the left and said: "You have been running the show for the past ten years, TODAY IS MY DAY!" He trashed his orderly files, threw bottles of colored inks on the ceiling, and was about to fling his personal computer out the window when his co-workers restrained him.

Sam was sent to a lovely place in the country for treatment. The most effective nondrug therapies there consisted of art therapy, music therapy, and sitting quietly while listening to the wind blow through the trees. After three months of feeding the parts of his brain that had been starving for all those years, Sam felt better. But on his first day back at work, he thought: I've missed three months of work. I'd better have coffee at my desk, a business lunch, take work home.

A few weeks later they took Sam away for good.

Sam's story illustrates a dramatic nervous breakdown. Many more people suffer mini-breakdowns in the course of everyday life. They scream irrationally at other drivers whose road manners do not meet with their approval. They come home from work and, without provocation, snap at their spouse, their children, or even their pets.

Many of us spend the majority of our days in a driven, focused mode, on the phone, at the computer terminal, or attending meetings. To avoid Sam's fate—to minimize mini-breakdowns, and to work the most productively and effectively—it is essential to take breaks.

Besides the usual bathroom and coffee breaks, make time for brain breaks. Take five or ten minutes, two or three times a day, to cultivate the balance of your hemispheres. Try listening to classical music, juggling, meditating, doing stretching exercises, practicing creative doodling, or playing daydreaming games.

Or take a walk outside. You'll return to work refreshed, more capable of seeing the big picture, better able to decide your priorities. Taking a brain break gives you the opportunity to metaphorically climb a tall tree and make sure you are cutting through the right jungle.

Moreover, research into the psychology of memory shows that taking regular breaks will improve your recall. If you study something for an hour and then take a break for ten minutes, your recall for the material you were studying will be higher *after* the break. This phenomenon is called the reminiscence effect. During breaks new information is digested, assimilated, and integrated with other memories, subconsciously. Appropriate breaks result in more efficient and effective learning and more productive work.

Perhaps you would like to take brain breaks but feel that your working environment is not conducive to such creative practices. Let's consider how to create an environment that supports the balanced brain.

CREATE A BRAIN-NOURISHING ENVIRONMENT

Where are you when you get your best ideas? Over the past fifteen years, I've asked thousands of people this question. Most people answer that they get their best ideas while resting in bed, driving in their cars, or relaxing in the shower or bath. Virtually no one says they get their best ideas at work.

What happens in the car, in bed, or in the shower that isn't happening in the workplace? Relaxation. Freedom from the fear of criticism. How can we create an atmosphere in the workplace that encourages the generation and application of our best ideas?

Consider the current state of most organizational environments.

Have you noticed the similarities among the designs of most corporate and government offices, hospitals, schools, and prisons? They usually feature cubicle structures, generic wall color, and fluorescent lights. This "cubicle consciousness" phenomenon is a symptom of "left-brain bias," which is based on the assumption that people work best in drab, uniform, linear environments, and that stark surroundings help us concentrate.

The sensory impressions from our daily environment act as a kind of food for our brain. Most people in the organizational world suffer from mental malnutrition, the result of a regular "junk-food diet" of sensory impressions.

Ironically, organizations everywhere are issuing urgent calls for greater creativity, innovation, and empowerment from all levels. Memos are sent, frantic speeches given, well-meaning meetings held, and nothing changes.

Regardless of whatever words are spoken, creativity and innovation must be nourished to become part of an organization's culture. This nourishment requires appropriate training in creative thinking, policy, and structure changes that reinforce desired behaviors and the development of environments that support the balanced brain.

As organizations demand greater creativity and innovation from their members, they must provide environments that encourage the behaviors they require. What are the keys to establishing an environment conducive to creativity? Let me tell you a few illustrative stories from my own experiences.

In 1982, the learning resources group of a medical equipment company asked for help in solving a training problem. This group was responsible for training customers to use and maintain a machine designed to conduct complex diagnostic tests. To remain cost-effective, training for this machine had to be completed within a week. The problem was that the training often took two or three weeks.

On my first visit to the site, I was impressed with the state-of-the-art interactive training technology. Students attended sophisticated computerized classes and had actual machines to work on. However, the learning environment was standard cubicle consciousness: generic color walls, fluorescent lights. The only attempt at aesthetics—large pictures of the machine hung just above each machine. The students were given one coffee break in the morning and one in the afternoon.

The thirty-nine members of the learning resources team spent three days on a training program, where they focused on the application of balanced-brain thinking skills to real-life problems. On the first day back in the workplace, the training facilitators experimented by playing classical music during the workday. From that first day on, they reported that their students were asking at least 50 percent fewer "unnecessary questions." They speculated that the music helped the students relax and focus, freeing them from the need to "get confused" in order to get a break from the monotony.

Among a number of other changes in the learning laboratory, they:

- Removed the machine pictures, and replaced them with Impressionist prints
- Replaced the fluorescent lights with full-spectrum bulbs
- Encouraged the students to bring in fresh flowers to make the environment more aesthetically pleasant and "alive"
- Transformed the coffee lounge into a "creative break room," filling it with colored pens and flip charts for doodling, toys, games, and juggling balls (the training supervisors had all learned to juggle)
- Encouraged the learners to take up to ten minutes of brain-break time every hour.

The learning resources group did its own study on the effects of these changes over the course of a year. The result: a 90 percent improvement in productivity.

In another instance, I conducted a "creative thinking" program for a group of engineers. Although their response to the program was positive, the engineers were not optimistic that they could apply what they had learned in their workplace. As they described it: "Our building is a giant cube. . . . The atmosphere is oppressive. . . . Music is out of the question. . . . If you use colored pens, you will be seen as childlike. . . . If you appear relaxed, they'll think you are goofing off."

After visiting their worksite, it was easy to empathize with their problem. The environment *was* oppressive. Their solution was to take over a conference room and transform it into a "team brain room." First, they replaced the furniture with comfortable chairs and a couch. They filled the room with flip charts and stocked it with colored pens. Then they brought in flowers and live plants, and hung inspiring art on the walls. They installed a stereo and assembled a collection of their favorite music. They topped it off by placing a stenciled name-plate on the wall outside the door. It read: BRAIN ROOM.

Thus, they legitimized a more balanced mode of functioning in the workplace, encouraging individual and team creativity.

Building a culture that supports balance and creativity in the work-place is a highly complex task. Creating your own brain room, however, is a simple, concrete step in the right direction. If you wish to create a brain room, consider the following elements and resources:

Room. Take a conference room, utility room, basement, or empty office and remove all standard furnishings and telephones. Put a sign on the door that says, CREATIVITY ROOM, BRAIN ROOM, THINK TANK, and so on.

Lighting. Natural lighting is best, so look for a room with windows. Replace standard fluorescent lights with UV radiation-protected-full-spectrum fluorescents, halogen lamps, or incandescent bulbs.

Sound. Install a good-quality stereo system and play classical music during brainstorming and breaks. (A recent study at the University of California demonstrated that I.Q. scores rise significantly, although temporarily, when subjects are tested while listening to Mozart.)

Aesthetics. Hang inspiring art on the walls and perhaps a mobile on the ceiling. Change the art every now and then to keep it fresh. Bring in living green plants and fresh flowers.

Furniture/Equipment. Bring in a comfortable couch, chairs, over-stuffed floor cushions, or even a hammock! Have an ample supply of flip charts (get the extra-large size if possible) and an abundance of colored pens and highlighters (water-based, nontoxic). Add an overhead projector (a good-quality, quiet model) and wall-size dry erase boards.

Feng Shui. This is an ancient Chinese system for arranging rooms, placing mirrors, screens, fountains, and furniture to balance the forces of yin and yang and maximize harmony with nature. Western companies such as Chase Manhattan, Citibank, Morgan Guaranty Trust, and innumerable organizations in the East employ Feng Shui consultants to create "brain-nourishing environments." You can do it yourself by consulting Sarah Rossbach's, *Interior Design With Feng Shui.* (It sounds weird but it really works.)

Air. Most indoor environments are stuffy and too hot or too cold. Have a heater/fan available. A humidifier, dehumidifier, or air purifier (green plants are helpful here) might be needed. Experiment with aromas—potpourri, incense, or essential oils (e.g., peppermint for alertness, lavender for relaxation).

Breaks. You may wish to have toys and games—modeling clay, Erector sets, juggling balls—available for breaks. You can also experiment with meditation/relaxation tapes.

Your Brain . . . is the most important ingredient in creating your BRAIN ROOM. Keep your mind open and committed to continuous improvement. Have fun working smarter!

Psychologists have known for many years that the quality of stimulation provided by the external environment is crucial to brain development in the early years of life. Brain researcher Dr. Richard Restak emphasizes that, "Throughout life, *not just during the first few months,* the brain's synaptic organization can be altered by the external environment." *Create a brain-nourishing environment at home. Take every opportunity to expose your senses to beauty. Turn your study, attic, or extra bedroom into a family brain room, and make sure that your children's study spaces are brain nourishing.*

KEEP A JOURNAL OR NOTEBOOK

Many creative people from all walks of life keep a journal or notebook, a place to record ideas, experiences, jokes, insights, sketches, poems, news items, quotes, and dreams. The free-flowing, unfinished, anything-goes quality of a personal journal encourages the playful open-mindedness that leads to insight. And, as you record things that inspire you, they are imprinted in your psyche at a deeper level. Remember to make a note of your best ideas. Keep a pen and notebook or dictation machine at places where you get your best ideas. If you record them, your output of good ideas will grow, along with the likelihood of actually applying them.

RECORD YOUR DREAMS

You may also wish to make a special point of recording your dreams. In a study at the University of British Columbia, students signed up for a course on dreaming. At the beginning of the term, they were given an extensive battery of creativity tests, followed by just one assignment: to record their dreams and discuss them with fellow students during class time. At the end of term, the students took another battery of creativity tests and their scores improved by more than 25 percent.

Bohr, Coleridge, Dali, Descartes (93), Jung (63), Poe, and many others point to dreams as the wellspring of their genius. Elias Howe, the inventor of the modern sewing machine, got the idea for putting the eye at the end of the needle, instead of the middle, from cannibals who were boiling him for supper in one of his dreams. The cannibals had little holes at the ends of their spears.

Remembering your dreams is easy.

- Before you go to sleep, say to yourself, "Tonight I will remember my dreams."
- Upon awakening, allow yourself to "drift" for a few minutes with your eyes closed, scanning your mind for pieces of your dreams.
- Note the elements of your dream in your journal or in a special dream diary. Do not expect them to make sense right away; just note down the images, scenes, key words, or phrases that the dream suggests.
- If you want to interpret your dream, pretend that you are talking to

the world's greatest psychiatrist and that she keeps asking you, "So tell me, what does this dream mean to you?"

TAKE TIME FOR SOLITUDE

In your waking hours, you can balance your brain by taking time for solitude. Most people experience their breakthrough ideas when they are by themselves. Solitude gives us the opportunity to "get our heads together." Take a little time each day to go for a walk by yourself. At least once a year, however hectic your life, get away by yourself for a couple of days. The intellectual and spiritual benefits of taking time alone will flow throughout the rest of your year.

APPRECIATE OTHERS WITH DIFFERENT BRAIN DOMINANCE

Taking time for solitude also will open the necessary "psychological space" for you to cultivate your appreciation for those who have a different brain dominance pattern. Take an artist or accountant to lunch. Aim to see the world from the point of view of someone who thinks differently from you, rather than judge others as flaky and weird, or nerdy and narrow. It's too easy to spend our lives surrounded by people from similar backgrounds who think in similar ways. Although this can be reassuring, it is not very stimulating to our creativity and growth. As significant as solitude is, it's also important to work creatively with others, preferably with those who have different styles of thinking. As you open your mind to unfamiliar perspectives you stretch and tone your synvergent muscles.

PURSUE YOUR IDEAL HOBBY

What are the things that you have always wanted to do or learn but never had the "time" to pursue?

I've asked thousands of people this question. The most common answers are: "to play a musical instrument . . . learn a new language . . . try scuba diving, sailing, or skydiving . . . play tennis or golf . . . learn to draw, paint, or sculpt . . . act in a play . . . sing in a choir . . . write poetry or novels . . . study dancing, yoga, or martial arts. . . ."

No one has ever responded, "I wish I had more free time for quantitative analysis." Most "ideal hobbies" are expressive, adventurous, or artistic activities—counterweights to the left-brain imbalance of many people's daily lives.

People who make their ideal hobbies real are much happier and more successful. They are, in Joseph Campbell's words, "following their bliss." By pursuing passionately an area of interest, besides work and family, they broaden their perspective in a way that enriches all aspects of their lives.

A vice president of a shipping company, after years of daydreaming about it, finally decided to pursue his ideal hobby of studying the martial art of aikido. He reflected, "Martial arts have taught me more about what's really important in being a manager than anything I studied in business school. I've stopped reacting defensively to criticism and learned that if I can keep my own balance intact that most conflict situations will resolve themselves. I'm used to being in charge so being a beginner was a real shock but it's really helped me understand and support my subordinates who are trying to master new processes and technologies. It's been a real eye-opener!"

PLAY GO

The ancient oriental game of Go has been used as a training tool for military and corporate strategists for centuries. It offers an intriguing, delightful way to cultivate synvergent thinking and balance your brain. A Go board is a 19" × 19" grid. Players alternate placing flying-saucer shaped "stones" (traditionally the black stones are made of flint, white from seashells) on the intersection points of the grid. Once a stone is placed on the board it cannot be moved. The object is to surround more space than your opponent. The rules are simple and you can begin playing Go with only a few minutes of instruction, although you can spend a lifetime exploring its complexities and aesthetics. Like chess, Go develops memory and analytical skill, but because the number of possible patterns is virtually unlimited, it pushes the aspiring adept to new depths of intuitive thinking. Progress at Go requires the ability to integrate big picture vision with exquisite attention to detail, nurturing the patterns emerging on the whole board while engaging in torrid tactical confrontations. And, the paradox of Go is that, more often than not, you win by knowing when and where to yield.

A traditional Go board.

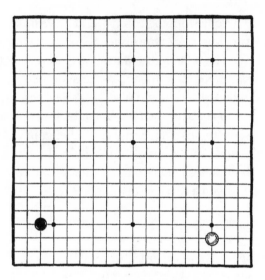

Go board viewed from above.

To get started read *Go for Beginners* (Ishi Press, Tokyo) by Kaoru Iwamoto.

PRACTICE MEDITATION

Meditation is an especially useful "hobby" for balancing your brain and nurturing the consciousness that makes transformation possible. In 1975, Dr. Bernard Glueck found that the brain wave patterns of meditators showed an increased harmony between the two hemispheres. Glueck concluded that meditation results in a stronger communication through the corpus callosum and greater coordination of the whole brain. Since then, a mounting body of evidence strongly suggests the benefit of meditative practices.

In his classic, *The Relaxation Response,* Dr. Herbert Benson reported on an in-depth scientific study of various styles of meditation and their psychological and physiological benefits. Benson found that regular meditation practice can help lower high blood pressure while counteracting the effects of everyday stress.

A simple but effective form of meditation takes just ten to twenty minutes. It's much easier if you create a quiet environment free from distractions, and if your stomach is closer to empty than full. Sit in a comfortable, upright position. Although it's possible to meditate lying down, you will probably fall asleep instead.

Approach meditation with a nonjudgmental, accepting attitude.

Begin by closing your eyes and scanning your body with your awareness. Gently bring your attention to your feet, then ankles, lower legs, knees, thighs, pelvis, lower back, upper back, stomach, chest, shoulders, upper arms, elbows, forearms, wrists, hands, fingers, face, neck, and head. As you attend briefly to each segment of your body, gently ask it to relax. Avoid waiting for a response or trying to relax. Just let it be and move on.

Next, bring your attention to the flow of your breathing, without trying to change it in any way. Sense the flow of your breath as the air comes in through your nostrils, fills your torso, and flows out through your nose or mouth. To quiet your mind and make it easier to enjoy the experience, you can repeat a word or phrase with each breath, such as *light* or *peace.* Each time you exhale, silently repeat the word.

Mind wandering is par for the course. Distracting thoughts are like birds flying around your head—you may not be able to stop them from fluttering about, but you can prevent them from roosting. When your mind wanders, as it will, bring your attention back to your repeated word and to the flow of your breathing. Maintain a laissez-faire attitude. Meditation is a natural, *effortless* function of your attention.

Meditation is not a means to an end. It is both the means and the end.
—J. Krishnamurti

DEVELOP PSYCHO-PHYSICAL FITNESS

The synvergent approach to fitness treats the body as an intelligent whole system, inseparable from the mind. It begins with a paradox: accept yourself as you are and train to improve, simultaneously.

Research in the new field of psycho-neuroimmunology demonstrates that our attitudes affect our physiology from moment to moment. Begin your psycho-physical fitness training by adopting a positive attitude based on this assumption: my body is a self-organizing, self-healing system that thrives with age (evidence supporting this assumption is provided by the work of Doctors Chopra, Dossey, Ornish, Siegel, and many others). Just as our attitudes have a profound affect on the body, the state of the body has a profound affect on the mind. Alertness, acuity, a feeling of well-being and mental stamina are all affected positively by appropriate fitness training.

Elements of psycho-physical fitness include: exercise, diet, rest, body awareness, and poise.

Exercise. Our bodies are designed for movement. Running, dancing, swimming, throwing, catching, lifting, and stretching are natural expressions of this design. Modern sedentary lifestyles necessitate making a special effort to allow this natural form of self-expression and health maintenance. A balanced exercise program develops aerobic capacity, strength, and flexibility.

• Aerobics—Dr. Kenneth Cooper, originator of the concept of aerobics, found that moderate exercise sustained for a period of twenty minutes, at least three times a week, has profoundly beneficial effects for the body and mind. Aerobic (with oxygen) exercise stengthens your cardiovascular system, improving blood and therefore oxygen flow to your body and brain. Your brain is, on average, less than 3 percent of your body's weight yet it uses more than 30 percent of your body's oxygen. *As you become aerobically fit you double your capacity to process oxygen.*

Cooper found that in addition to the cardio-vascular benefits, subjects maintaining a regular program of aerobic exercise experience significant improvements in alertness, emotional stability and are less susceptible to fatigue. Moreover, regular aerobic exercise stimulates your metabolism improving digestion and regulating weight. The key to a successful aerobic fitness program is to find an activity, or combination of activities, that you *enjoy.*

• Strength—Competitive athletes know that strength training is a key to high performance. But weightlifting is also valuable for those seeking optimum wellness. It is an efficient method for burning unnecessary body fat while cultivating muscle tone and resilience. Weight training improves the strength of connective tissue and bone as well as muscle. Physical strength and lively muscle tone support the capacity for focused attention and mental stamina. World chess champion Gary Kasparov trains for the ultimate mental combat by running, boxing, and weight lifting. Body building legend Arnold Schwarzenegger emphasizes that effective weight training is primarily a discipline of visualization and focused attention. To begin a strength training program find a good coach or trainer and seek guidance on developing proper form. And remember, no brain, no gain.

• Flexibility—Stretching benefits your circulatory and immune systems while preventing injury and optimizing the joy of movement. Practice simple stretching exercises before and after aerobic and strength training, upon arising, and every now and then throughout your day. The secret to a good stretch is to take your time, bring your full awareness to the process, and allow easy release of muscle groups in harmony with extended exhalations. Never bounce or try to force a stretch. Hatha yoga offers the most sophisticated approach to stretching.

Diet. Diet fads come and go but there are a few common sense guidelines for healthy eating that stand the test of time. To live a balanced life, eat a balanced diet. Seek food that is fresh, wholesome, and aesthetically pleasing. Eat plenty of fiber, drink at least eight glasses of pure water each day, and moderate your intake of salt, sugar, fat, red meat, caffeine, and alcohol. Most importantly, listen to your body and determine what you actually want to eat. If in doubt, imagine how you will feel *after* you eat the food in question. Then, pause for a few moments before eating and bring your awareness to the present moment. Savor the smell, taste, and texture of every bite. And, enjoy every meal.

Rest. Disasters such as Three Mile Island, Chernobyl, and the Challenger explosion all have one element in common: fatigued workers were too exhausted to make appropriate judgments that could have prevented these, and many other tragedies. Accidents caused by insufficent rest and overwork, according to Dr. Martin Moore-Ede author of *The Twenty-Four Hour Society,* cost the global economy more than $80 billion per year. In the organizational world, exhaustion has become a way of life. When I ask my corporate classes if they suffer from fatigue, many are too tired to respond. Fourteen-hour work days are not uncommon. Many profess a perverse pride in overwork, boasting about their long hours and the number of years they have gone without a vacation. If you are working intensely, for the sake of quality work and life, it is essential to *discipline* yourself to get adequate rest. Enjoy your full vacation time every year. Discover the amount of sleep you need to feel rested and invigorated, then follow a regular schedule of retiring and arising.

In addition to vacations, regular sleep, taking brain breaks and practicing meditation. (Meditation functions as concentrated rest. Research shows that twenty minutes of meditation provides physiological benefits equivalent to almost two hours of sleep.) You can optimize your daily performance by taking power naps. Power naps are the stamina secret of many high performers including Napoleon, Thomas Edison (11), Salvador Dali (36), industrialists John D. Rockefeller and Armand Hammer, and Presidents Teddy Roosevelt, John Kennedy, Ronald Reagan, and Bill Clinton. As Winston Churchill urged: "Nature had not intended man to work from eight in the morning until midnight without the refreshment of blessed oblivion, which, even if it lasts only twenty minutes, is sufficient to renew all vital forces."

Body Awareness and Poise. How do you know when you are stressed? Of course, your body informs you. Some people know from a nuance of neck tension or a tight stomach, others don't figure it out until they develop a stress-related ailment. Body awareness is the first step in self-awareness and a key to true fitness. Sensitivity to bodily feelings and sensations provides crucial information for knowing and responding to your true needs. Zen masters teach that a key to well-being and enlightenment is "eat when hungry, sleep when tired." Yet, frequently the pace of our lives and the intensity of the external assault on our senses drowns out the sometimes subtle messages our bodies provide. Regular exercise, a healthy diet, and adequate rest will set the stage for you to become more sensitive and attuned to yourself.

Body awareness is also the key to cultivating poise, the missing link in many fitness programs. Poise is the balanced distribution of energy in the body. Exercise without poise often does more harm than good. Slumping runners and contorted weight lifters, for example, create what philosopher John Dewey called "compensatory maladjustments," distorting the whole system to produce a specific result. The key to poise and high performance in many activities is the synvergent state of relaxed concentration. The most effective way to learn relaxed concentration is the technique developed in 1896 by Australian actor F. M. Alexander (66 in the Buzan/Keene genius hall of fame).

Alexander discovered that whenever we move or speak, most of us tend to shorten and stiffen the muscles of the neck thereby interfering with the balance of the head. The average head weighs ten to fifteen pounds and if it is off balance it causes a pattern of contraction that compresses the spine and throws the whole body out of alignment. Misalignment places undue pressure on internal organs, it impedes breathing, and disturbs coordination. Alexander found that this pattern of contraction and misalignment begins with *just the thought of moving or speaking.*

Lessons in the Alexander technique guide you to change your thinking so you can outwit this contraction pattern. As you emancipate yourself from this unnecessary tension habit, you experience an increasingly delightful sense of balance and relaxed concentration in all your activities. Alexander work will lead you to subtle, profound insights into the inseparable nature of mind and body, forming an experiential framework for appreciating wholeness and nurturing synvergent thinking. Appropriate training in the technique requires the assistance of a qualified teacher (contact The North American Society of Teachers of the Alexander Technique at 1-800-473-0620).

CULTIVATE AMBIDEXTERITY

In 1980, Tony Buzan and I interviewed Prof. Raymond Dart, the renowned anthropologist and anatomist. We asked Professor Dart to describe his most important discovery in a lifetime of studying human development. He jumped up from his chair and exclaimed, "You must go out and tell people to balance their brains, balance their bodies. The future lies with the ambidextrous human!"

Ambidexterity offers another avenue to psycho-physical fitness and life balance. You can cultivate your ambidexterity by experimenting with reversing your hand dominance. Practice interlocking your fingers and crossing your arms and legs in reverse of your normal pattern. Eat lunch and brush your teeth with your "other" hand. See if you can wink your nondominant eye. Try learning to juggle—Professor Dart specifically prescribes this as a way to balance mind and body.

Experiment, as Leonardo da Vinci did, by writing with both hands at once in different directions. Try geometrical shapes, letters of the alphabet, writing your name.

Jack Fincher, author of *Lefties*, describes a brilliant example of creative ambidexterity, applied by famed attorney Louis Nizer. You may wish to emulate and adapt this to your own purposes.

> Nizer, a right-hander, has long had the habit of casually, aimlessly, all but unconsciously sketching jurors with his left hand while listening to testimony. Such sketches, he finds, give him surprising and useful insights into the personality and character of those upon whom his client's fate depends. So effective have such intuitions proven in tailoring his presentation and summary that Nizer keeps a file of the sketches.

Complement your ambidexterous endeavors with **ambidextrous breathing.** You can cultivate brain balance by practicing a technique based on ancient yogic wisdom and modern scientific understanding: alternate-nostril breathing.

Research shows that left-nostril breathing stimulates the right brain and vice versa. By alternating from left to right you inspire hemispheric coherence. Sit in an upright position, close your eyes and then begin by blocking the flow of air into your right nostril by depressing it with your thumb or index finger as you exhale slowly through the left, then, inhale through your left. Now, close off your left nostril and exhale slowly through your right side. Keep the left blocked and inhale through the right. Then, exhale through the left, inhale through the left, exhale through the right and so on. Try this alternate-nostril breathing for up to three minutes at a time, twice a day. Avoid forcing or holding your breath. If you feel dizzy or uncomfortable in any way, stop. Most people find that this practice is both calming and energizing.

ENCOURAGE "BOTH SIDES" OF YOUR CHILDREN

On the second day of a High Performance Learning Center seminar for a New York bank, an executive vice president commented, "You know, I've been a fool. I have two kids; one is just like me—very good at math and figures, disciplined, and focused. My other kid is totally different—a real dreamer, very artistic but all over the place. Last night I realized that I have been discriminating against my more right-brained child. If I were more open to him and encouraged him to share his way of looking at things with his brother and me, then we would all be better off!"

Just as we must build teams with balanced brains in the workplace, we must also do so at home. Many parents pass on half-witted prejudices to their children. Support your kids in developing the skills of logic and imagination together. If your child shows a preference for right-brain thinking, tackle history lessons by acting out scenes from the past. Approach mathematics by writing out theorems and equations in bold colors. Help your child be on time by making a color-coded, picture-filled calendar. If your child's orientation is more left brained, help him or her to be more balanced by emphasizing art, drama, and music appreciation.

TRANSCEND SEXUAL STEREOTYPES

The left brain is frequently associated with a more traditionally "male" mode—analytical, focused, convergent. This is the mode for influencing the environment, for getting things done, for *doing*. On the other hand, the right hemisphere is often associated with the more traditionally female mode—receptive, intuitive, divergent. This is the mode for sensitivity to the environment, for letting things be, for *being*. To be whole, we must integrate the masculine and feminine principles.

Oriental wisdom has long recognized that the balance of yin and yang, of being *and* doing, is a prerequisite for enlightenment. In the West, the importance of this integration is becoming apparent through research. In a landmark study at Stanford University, psychologists discovered that the highest levels of intellectual functioning are incompatible with stereotypes of masculinity and femininity. Dr. E. P. Torrance found that gender stereotypes inhibit creativity. Torrance discovered that creativity requires a balance between sensitivity, traditionally a female trait, and autonomy, a trait usually associated with males.

The synvergent approach, integrating masculine and feminine principles, is more than just a key to individual creativity and fulfillment. It is a social and cultural imperative. As intellectual historian Dr. Richard Tarnas concludes in *The Passion of the Western Mind,* the Western psyche is on the verge of an unprecedented epochal transformation: "a triumphant and healing . . . reconciliation between the two great polarities, a union of opposites: a sacred marriage between the long-dominant but now alienated masculine and the long-suppressed but now ascending feminine."

HAVE YOUR CAKE AND EAT IT, TOO

There are two kinds of people:
those who divide everything into two groups,
and those who don't.
—Kenneth Boulding

Practice thinking synvergently. Move beyond compartmentalized, either/or ways of looking at yourself and the world. Embrace the paradoxes of everyday life. Be a planner and an improviser. Balance substance and process, seriousness and play. Seek the synergetic integration of intuition and analysis, leadership and management, left brain and right brain, male and female.

In 1980, Tony Buzan and I were flying from England to New England to lead a seminar together. Our client generously provided us with first-class passage. After a sumptuous meal, the flight attendant came around with a dessert cart, asking passengers if they would prefer a chocolate gateau or an ice cream creation. When she asked Tony, he smiled and, with a twinkle in his eye, said, "Both, please." At first the attendant was taken aback, but then her expression softened into a smile. "Of course, sir."

Would you care for a thriving economy, or do you prefer a viable environment?

Can I interest you in advancing technology, or maybe instead you'd like to develop human resources?

Would you like to be rich and successful, or would you prefer to serve humanity?

Both, please.

A basic understanding of synvergent thinking, conscious optimism, and brain-balancing practices has set the stage. Now you are ready to learn a whole new approach to generating and organizing ideas. Earlier in this chapter we learned that according to Professor Anokhin of Moscow University, your potential for association and idea generation is virtually unlimited. What if there were a practical method for unleashing this potential? What if you could use this method to freely access, organize, and record new patterns of association, quickly and enjoyably?

The method exists. It is called mind mapping. In the next chapter, I will show you how to use mind mapping to unleash your vast power of creative association and to awaken your synvergent intelligence.

Chapter 2

Mind Mapping: The Self-Organizing Nature of Intelligence

Think about the last book you read or the last seminar you attended. Imagine that you have to write a report on that book or seminar. Begin recalling the information. As you do, observe the process of your mind at work. Does your mind work by constructing whole paragraphs, by presenting ordered outlines to your mind's eye? Probably not. Chances are that impressions, key words, and images float into mind, one associating with the next. Mind mapping is a method for continuing this natural thinking process on paper.

Mind mapping originated as a tool for note taking and note making. Note taking focuses on recording someone else's thoughts, as from a book, lecture, seminar, or meeting. Note making is for generating, organizing, and integrating your own thoughts and for fully incorporating the thoughts that you've learned through note taking into your own thinking process.

Although mind mapping is used in a wide variety of specific applications including strategic planning, presentation design and delivery, academic study, and creative problem solving, its greatest value comes from its power to train you to think synvergently.

Create a Positive Feedback Loop

Mind mapping is based on the assumption that our notes are manifestations of our thinking. If we manifest our thoughts in harmony with the natural functioning of the mind, we think better. In other words, mind mapping works by creating a positive feedback loop between your brain and your notes. Mind mapping trains you to manifest your thoughts in a way that makes it easier to see the whole picture and the details, to integrate logic and imagination. It encourages a synergetic integration of convergent and divergent thinking. By allowing you to capture a tremendous amount of information on one piece of paper, mind mapping helps you see the relationships, connections, and patterns of your ideas. Regular practice of mind mapping trains you to look at your job, your family, yourself, and your world in a more synvergent, systems-oriented manner.

To thrive in our chaotic age we must develop our ability to understand patterns of change, to see the web of connections that underlie complex systems. Mind mapping is a simple process that can help you manage complexity and understand patterns of change. It is a tool for mastering the big amoeba.

Beyond the Outline

Most of us grew up learning to express and organize our thoughts by making outlines. The traditional outline begins with "roman numeral one." Have you ever spent an inordinate amount of time waiting for idea I?

Perhaps you finally get idea roman numeral I after twenty minutes or so, and you continue your outline down to point IIId when you realize that point IIId should be point IIb. You cross it out and draw an arrow. Now your outline is getting messy. And we all know that outlines must be *neat*. Perhaps you become distracted by this mess and start to doodle or daydream. Your repressed right brain tries to express itself through doodling and daydreaming, but with the doodling, your outline is even messier, and you feel guilty for daydreaming. So you crumple up your paper and start again.

Outlining is a reflection of a hierarchical mind-set. Although valuable as a tool for presenting ideas in a formal, orderly fashion, *it is useful only after the real thinking has been done.* If you try to generate your ideas by outlining, you will find that it slows you down and stifles your freedom of thought. It is just plain illogical to try to organize your ideas before you've generated them.

Moreover, outlining and other traditional note-making systems exclude your brain's capacity for color, dimension, synthesis, rhythm, and image. By imposing one color and one form, outlining guarantees monotony. Outlining uses only half of your mind, and half a mind is a terrible thing to waste.

Mind mapping frees you from the tyranny of premature organization. Premature organization stifles generation. Mind mapping liberates your conceptual powers by balancing generation and organization, convergence and divergence, while encouraging the full range of mental expression.

Mind Mapping: Streams of Development

Before you learn how to mind map, let's consider its origin and development. Mind mapping was originated by my colleague, Tony Buzan. Since 1975, we have been working together to refine the discipline and to develop new strategies for teaching it. State-of-the-art mind mapping is based on the confluence of the following streams of research and understanding:

Mind mapping is based on research into note-taking skills.

In the late 1960s, Tony Buzan worked at the College of Advanced Reading in England, where he taught speed-reading and study skills to students while he researched methods for improving learning, memory, and creative thinking. He did an extensive study of various note-taking styles, aiming to discover what would work best for his students.

Drawing on the research of Prof. Michael Howe, at Exeter University, Buzan concluded that the best note takers shared two distinctive characteristics. First, they used key words. Key words are the nuggets of creative association and recall. They are information rich. If you think of a key word, it inspires other key associations.

For instance, if you are studying Shakespeare, a key word might be *Hamlet*. If you think of Hamlet, chances are you'll have a rich series of associations, such as: prince, Denmark, Polonius, Elsinore. Non-key words might include *and* or *the*.

Once we learn grammar and syntax, our minds automatically "grammatize" our thoughts, so it's rarely necessary to record all those *and's*, *the's*, and *of's* that link key words. Your mind does this automatically. Time and energy spent recording and memorizing non-key words is wasted.

Professor Howe's other important finding was that the best note takers keep their notes clear and easy to read. Many students suffer from an inability to read their own handwriting, making their note-taking efforts useless. Tony Buzan also found that the best note takers take the time to print their notes. Printing, in addition to making the notes easier to read, *imprints* the key thought more clearly in the mind of the note taker.

Mind mapping is based on the psychology of memory.

To improve on printed key word notes, Buzan drew on his research into the psychology of memory, focusing on the two key elements of recall: association and emphasis. He began to brainstorm, "How can I bring more association and emphasis to printed, key word notes?"

You can "rediscover" mind mapping for yourself by considering Buzan's questions:

How can key words be graphically associated to show the linking of ideas? Well, you could connect them with lines and arrows. You could use codes or colors to show relationship.

What about emphasis? How can relative importance be simply illustrated. Obviously, you could use SIZE, **boldness**, UPPER- and lowercase letters, symbols (°$#@!˜), and pictures.

Is it possible to use symbols for association? Can you use colors for emphasis? Of course. Anything that creates more association can be used to create better emphasis and vice versa.

Mind mapping is based on an understanding of networks and natural systems.

Contemplate the structure of a tree; it is a network of life, expanding in all directions from its trunk, its center. Take a helicopter ride over a major city; it is a sprawling structure of interconnecting centers and pathways, main arteries connecting with side roads. Our global telecommunication system and solar system are similarly linked networks. The structure of communication in nature is nonhierarchical and self-organizing, it works through networks and systems. The ability to read, align, and work creatively with these systems is ultimately the definition of intelligence.

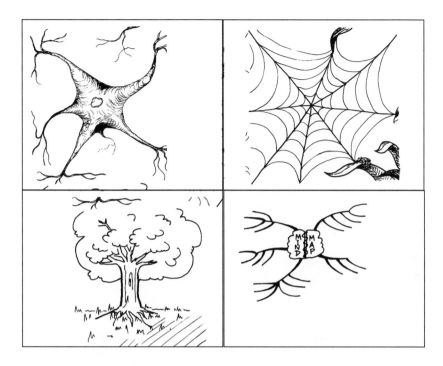

Brain cells, spiderwebs, trees, and mind maps all express the same natural pattern.

Mind mapping is based on an understanding of the structure and function of the brain.

All knowledge bears the imprint of the mind's own structure.
—Stephen Toulmin, brain researcher

Perhaps the most amazing natural system of all is right inside your skull. The basic structural unit of brain function is the neuron. Each of our billions of neurons branches out from a center, called the nucleus. Each branch, or dendrite (from *dendron*, meaning "tree"), is covered with little nodes called dendritic spines. As we think, electrochemical information jumps across the tiny gap between spines. This junction is called a synapse. Our thinking is a function of a vast network of synaptic patterns. A mind map is a graphic expression of these natural patterns of the brain.

As the exercise at the beginning of this chapter shows, our minds don't operate naturally through outlines and paragraphs. They work best when we integrate all of our higher capabilities in a way that reflects the synergy of the two hemispheres. Mind mapping integrates the left-brained, convergent aspects of our mind's functioning: logic, language, mathematical reasoning, attention to detail, sequence, ordering, and analysis, with the more right-brained divergent elements: dimensionality, rhythm, color, picture, symbols, imagination, and synthesis. Mind mapping "rescues" these right-brain elements, previously relegated to the realm of doodling and daydreaming, making them a productive part of our thinking and problem solving.

Mind mapping is based on what your mind really wants to do.

Many creative people have developed a branching, image-rich, keyword-oriented note-taking style. Entrepreneur and author Rebel Holiday demonstrates a mind map way of thinking as she describes her decision-making process: "First I think of all my choices, even ones I would never do. Then I pretend that I am standing at the base of a tree and *I follow the ideas out to the ends of all the branches,* and then I see how it looks and feels when I am there. Seeing the whole tree of ideas, the solution becomes obvious."

In the late 1980s Jim D'Agostino was pouring concrete for a living. Today he is president of billion-dollar construction giant Lehrer McGovern Bovis. After seeing a mind mapping demonstration for the first time, he exclaimed, "That's the way my brain works . . . that's what I've always been trying to do on my own!"

The note-taking styles of many of history's great brains such as Charles Darwin (30), Michelangelo (5), Leonardo da Vinci (1), and Mark Twain, feature a networked, branching structure, lots of creative doodles, sketches, and key words. The genius of Buzan's creation of mind mapping is his integration and formalization of what the mind naturally wants to do.

The Elements of Mind Mapping

The elements of mind mapping are based on an integration of the information just presented on effective note taking, the nature of memory, observation of nature, a practical understanding of the structure and design of the human brain, and study of the thinking patterns of great brains.

1. Begin your mind map with a **symbol** ***or a*** **picture** ***at the center of your page.***

Starting at the center rather than at the top of the page helps to free you from the limitations of hierarchical, "top-down" thinking. It opens your mind to a full 360 degrees of association. Pictures and symbols are much easier to remember than words and enhance your ability to think creatively about your subject. Your drawing will serve as the home base for your creative associations. Don't worry if you think you can't draw, just do the best you can. You can get the "brain benefits" without being a Renoir or Georgia O'Keefe.

2. Use key words. Key words are the information-rich nuggets of recall and creative association. They are easier to remember than sentences or phrases. Key words can be generated faster than sentences or phrases, without sacrificing meaning. Moreover, training yourself to look for key words enhances your ability to get to the essence of your material.

3. Connect the key words with lines radiating from your central image. By linking words with lines (branches), you'll show clearly how one key word relates to another. Connect the lines for maximum clarity.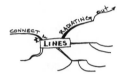

4. Print your key words. Printing is easier to read and remember than writing.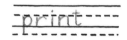

5. Print one key word per line. By doing this, you free yourself to discover the maximum number of creative associations for  each key word. The discipline of one word per line also trains you to focus on the most appropriate key word, enhancing the precision of your thought and minimizing clutter. This combination of focused and flexible thinking strengthens your synvergent powers.

6. Print your key words on the lines and make the length of the word the same as the line it is on. This maximizes clarity of association and encourages economy of space. (You will need plenty of space because you will be generating ideas faster than ever!) Avoid letting your key words "float" off the lines. This graphic disconnection short-circuits the flow of association.

7. Use colors, pictures, dimension, and codes for greater association and emphasis. Highlight important points and show relationships between different 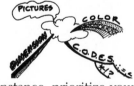 branches of your mind map. You might, for instance, prioritize your main points through color-coding, highlighting in yellow the most important points, using blue for secondary points, and so forth.

Pictures and images, preferably in vivid color, should be used wherever possible; they stimulate your creative association and greatly enhance your memory. Codes, such as asterisks, exclamation points, letters, shapes, and numbers, can be used to show relationships between concepts and to serve as tools to further organize your map.

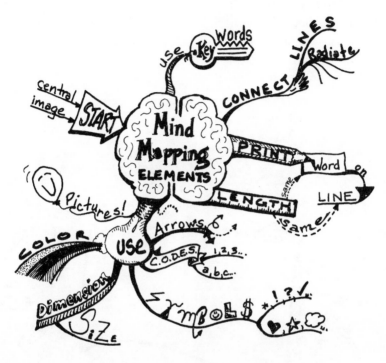

A mind map of the elements of mind mapping.

PUTTING THE ELEMENTS TO WORK

Mind mapping is simple and easy. You don't need much to begin—just your brain, a piece of paper, a few colored pens, and a willingness to learn something new.

Try making a mind map. Follow these instructions.

1. Begin with a large sheet of blank white paper and six or more colored pens. You may want to use phosphorescent highlighters for extra

color. Of course, one pen or pencil and a small sheet of paper will work in a pinch.

Although you can make mind maps on the back of matchbooks, in the palm of your hand, or on Post-it Notes, it's best to use a big sheet of paper; flip-chart size is recommended. The bigger the paper, the greater the freedom to express your associations. Place the paper horizontally in front of you. A horizontal disposition makes it easier for you to keep all your key words upright and easy to read.

2. Let's say that the topic for this mind map is "Living a Balanced Life."

Start your mind map by drawing a representative image in the middle of the paper. It doesn't matter if the image is abstract, symbolic, or concrete, as long as it reminds you of your topic. Draw it as vividly as you can, using more than one color. Have fun and don't worry about the accuracy of your drawing.

*This central image represents the integration of body ▽, emotions ♥, two hemispheres of the brain, and spirit *.*

3. Now, print key words or images on lines radiating out from your central image. Remember to print on the lines, one key word or image per line, and keep the lines connected.

Generating ideas in key-word form is easy. For example, as you think about living a balanced life, one key word might be FAMILY, which might trigger other key word associations, like LOVE, NEEDS, RESPONSIBILITIES. Another key branch could be HEALTH, triggering associations such as EXERCISE, REST, DIET. Other main branches might include CAREER, FINANCES, SPIRITUALITY, COMMUNITY, HOBBIES.

If you feel stuck, choose any key word on your mind map and immediately print your first association with that word—even if it seems ridiculous or irrelevant. Keep your associations flowing and don't worry about making sure that every word is "right."

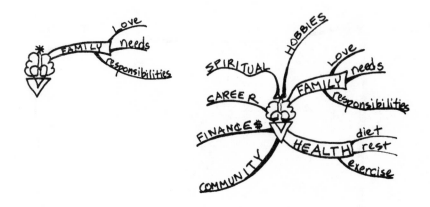

4. When you feel you have generated enough material through free association, look at the result: all your ideas spread across one page. As you examine your mind map, you will see relationships that help you organize and integrate your ideas. Look for words that appear repeatedly throughout the map. They often suggest major themes.

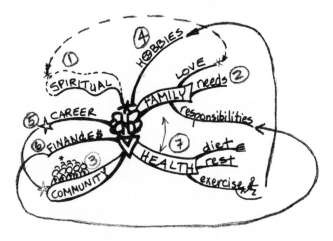

5. Connect related parts of your mind map with arrows, codes, and colors. Eliminate elements that seem extraneous. Pare your mind map down to just the ideas you need for your purpose. Then put them in sequence, if necessary. This can be accomplished with numbers or by redrawing the mind map in clockwise order.

The Top Twenty Questions and Answers About Mind Mapping

These are the most common questions people ask about mind mapping.

Q: I find it difficult to express my ideas in pictures. Is it really necessary?

A: Yes. Pictures serve as "memory anchors" for your key word associations. Research by Haber, Standing, Nickerson, and others show that pictures are much more memorable than words. When trying to recall your mind map, the first things you are likely to remember are the pictures.

Pictures also serve to "jump-start" the more imaginative aspect of your thinking, enhancing your creative output. Let yourself draw "as a child" without judgment of artistic merit. For many people, drawing pictures and symbols requires awakening a part of the brain that has been dormant for decades. Many of us are artistically illiterate. Unless you demonstrated special talent, chances are that you had your last art lesson when you were ten or eleven years old. Can you imagine if we treated other subjects in this manner—"Sorry, you don't show any special talent for history so we're cutting you off at the Middle Ages."

As our overview of great brains and discussion of Sperry's Nobel Prize–winning research in the previous chapter suggests, the imaginative and artistic aspects of thinking are essential to high performance. So, even if they seem awkward or unrecognizable at first, start drawing symbols and pictures in your mind maps. As you practice, your imagination, playfulness, and recall will expand accordingly. And, of course, your drawing will improve.

Q: Would you give some guidance in drawing symbols and pictures?

A: Try these simple drawings and symbols. They're all based on simple circles, squares, triangles, and lines (see pages 62–63).

Q: Is it really necessary to print only one word on each line?

A: With a few exceptions, yes. Printing one word per line keeps your mind map clear and easy to read. The discipline of one word per line trains you to focus on the most appropriate key word, enhancing the precision of your thought. At the same time, it leaves you free to find the maximum number of associations with each key word, increasing the freedom, breadth, and spontaneity of your thought.

Q: What about quotations, set phrases, or long formulas?

A: These are the exceptions. When you have a quotation, phrase, formula, or other piece of information that needs to be recorded verba-

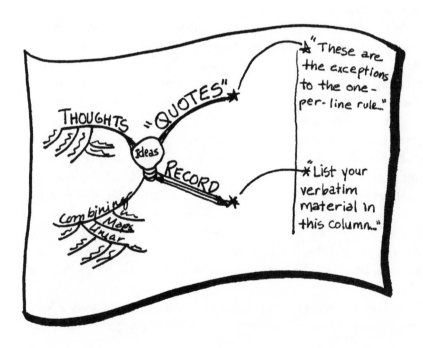

tim, do this: create a column along one side of your sheet, then list your verbatim material in this column with an arrow connecting to the relevant part of your mind map. This is a common strategy of students preparing for exams.

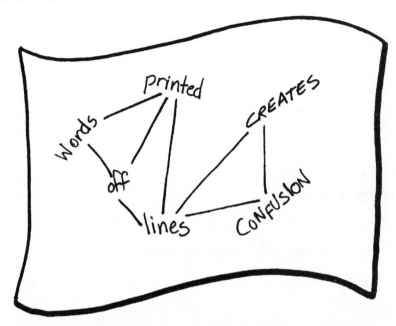

Q: Do I really have to connect the lines?

A: Yes. Disconnected lines mirror disconnected thoughts. Connecting the lines keeps your thoughts more connected by clarifying the path of association between words.

Q: Is it better to use different colors right from the beginning, or to add them later after pouring out my basic ideas in one color first?

A: Some people prefer to change colors as they open new branches, finding that different colors inspire them to generate ideas faster and more freely. Others feel that this slows them down. They prefer to create a multicolored central image and use one base color to generate ideas, applying different colors *afterward* as a way to organize and integrate the mind map. Experiment with both approaches and discover which works best for you.

SYMBOLS are Meaning-Rich (FUN) and EASY to DRAW!

First, start with some basics:

! ? * # ♡ $ + – √ ∅ = ≠ / « » ♭ ∧ X ÷ √

∞ , · ; : □ △ ¥ £ ¢ [ ] ( ) < > ≤ ≥ ⊥ % ≡

+ ≈ ∈ √ ∫ ♀ ♂ † ∩ C U Σ ± ♪ ⊙

You can draw arrows...

Rectangles, Squares, & Triangles are your building BLOCKS...

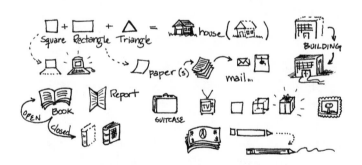

Throw in some curves!

Now draw some circles...

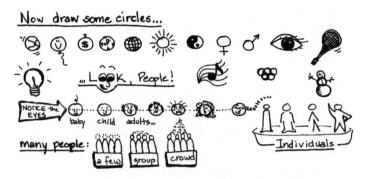

Try these simplified symbols:

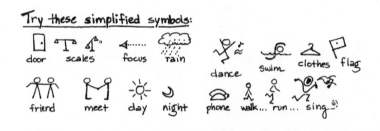

door scales focus rain dance swim clothes flag

friend meet day night phone walk... run... sing

Now let's combine the elements further...

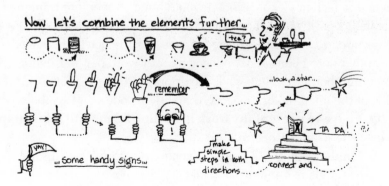

Q: How can I avoid printing upside down?

A: Use angled and curved lines as necessary in order to keep all your key words upright and easy to read.

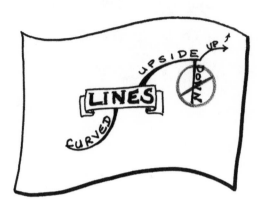

Q: What's the difference between mind mapping and other note-taking systems such as clustering, spider diagrams, idea mapping, and decision trees?

A: These various methods have one point in common with mind mapping: they are all nonlinear methods to generate and record thoughts. Mind mapping, however, is the only one that encourages you to take full advantage of all your brain's abilities. Mind mapping is based on the assumption that your thinking process can be improved by taking and making notes in a brain-friendly fashion. It's specifically designed to facilitate expression of whole-brain, synvergent thinking by creating a positive feedback loop between your notes and your brain. It encourages a more precise and organized approach to thinking than any other note-taking system (using one key word per line, connected lines, numbering, coding) while incorporating the imaginative, artistic side of the mind (color, imagery, dimension, codes, and symbols).

Q: I have to present my work in outline form. Will mind maps cause me to be disorganized?

A: Mind mapping will help you generate outlines quickly and easily. At first glance, mind maps may appear messy, but they lead to greater thought organization and are easily translated into outlines.

Mind mapping lets you generate your ideas faster and more freely and then organize them with a greater range of organizational tools (colors, numbers, codes). If you require an outline, simply assign a roman numeral to each branch of your mind map and a letter code to each key word.

Q: How can I keep my mind map neat, organized, and easy to work with?

A: Keep your central image in the center of the page and limit its size. Use just one word per line and be sure to print the key words. Make the lines a bit thicker at their origin and print your letters at least one-quarter inch in height so they are easy to read. You can print some letters even larger for emphasis. Make each word the same size as the line underneath it. This saves space and allows you to see connections more clearly.

If possible, use large sheets of paper. This helps to avoid crowding and encourages you to think big. Do not be concerned if your first draft seems disorganized. You can make a second or third draft for further clarification.

Q: How do you know that your mind map is finished?

A: Theoretically, a mind map never ends. As Leonardo da Vinci emphasized, "Everything is connected to everything else." If you had the time, energy, inclination, enough colored pens, and a big enough piece of paper, you could go on linking all your knowledge and ultimately all human knowledge. Of course, if you are planning a speech or organizing a meeting, you probably don't have time to link all human knowledge. The simple answer is that your mind map is finished when the information you have generated meets your objectives for the task at hand.

Q: If a thought seems silly or irrelevant, should I leave it out?

A: If an idea seems silly or irrelevant, put it down and keep the process flowing. Breakthrough ideas often begin with associations that initially seem off the wall. If a key word ultimately seems irrelevant, you can always eliminate it in the second edition of your mind map.

Q: I seem to have a problem determining what goes on the main branches of my mind map. Are there guidelines to help me?

A: Yes. Aim to discover the minimum number of key words that best summarize the subject of your central image. Do a generative, free-flowing map first, then determine your main branches using the above criteria. You can also determine main branches by beginning with obvious logical divisions of your material. If you are mind mapping a book, for example, your major branches will usually become the chapter or section titles. A speech can be branched according to the formula—beginning, middle, and end, or you could use your seven key points. Another approach is to use the classic questions: who, what, when, where, why, and how?

The important thing is that you do not let your concern for the "right" categories interfere with the flow of your thoughts—*it is the flow that helps you discover the categories.* In other words, the first time you make a mind map on a given topic, do not worry about what goes where. Just allow your associations to flow, then survey your map and highlight your strongest key words. In your *second* edition of the mind map you can make those key words your main branches.

Q: I want to customize mind mapping and develop my own style. What do you advise?

A: The elements of mind mapping are designed to encourage individual self-expression. Each of these guidelines has been carefully developed and tested to help you maximize your thinking skill over the long term. For at least the first six weeks, apply the elements exactly as presented. Then experiment with customizing them.

Imitate, Assimilate, Innovate—advice on learning how to play jazz, master martial arts, and become adept at mind mapping

Q: How can I introduce mind mapping to others without giving a long-winded discourse on brain research?

A: The best way to share mind mapping with others is to show them one of your mind maps and explain the content. You need not mention the brain or even the term "mind mapping." Just use your mind map to illustrate the flow of your thinking. The natural logic of the process makes it readily accessible.

After capturing their interest, share the elements and guide them through an exercise in mind mapping a project, vacation, speech, homework assignment, or daily plan. Then encourage them to read the literature, listen to the audiotapes and view the videotapes that are available, and ideally, attend a course from a qualified instructor.

Q: I am concerned about using mind maps in the workplace. Won't people think it's childish to play with colored pens?

A: This is a common initial reaction. Once they overcome their surprise at seeing something different, most people are receptive to anything that can make their work easier and more effective. Apply the approach described in the answer to the previous question and this concern will disappear.

Q: Do people really use mind mapping?

A: When people are properly taught to use mind mapping, they apply it immediately and continuously in their professional and personal lives. Mind mapping has become an essential tool used on a daily basis in large segments of Fortune 500 companies, as well as by many other individuals and organizations. It will become a standard operating procedure of the schools and companies of the twenty-first century.

Q: What about mind mapping software?

A: A number of mind mapping software programs have been developed in recent years. Although still relatively slow and inflexible compared to the traditional pen and paper method, computers offer a number of advantages including: vast storage, easy filing, quick retrieval, and relatively flawless reproduction capacity. Imminent, exciting software developments include: on-line group mind mapping, offering wonderful opportunities for team problem solving; more flexible graphics for central and other images; and, pen pad technology, integrating the advantages of traditional mind mapping with the benefits of the computer. Someday there will be voice recognition and holographic technology for the ultimate synthesis of brain and computer.

Q: What are the advantages of mind mapping?

A: As you experiment with mind mapping, its advantages will become increasingly obvious. Mind mapping gives you easier access to your brain's potential. It allows you to start quickly and generate more ideas in less time. Its free-ranging format—adding words to one branch one moment, then skipping over to another branch the next—increases your chances of generating new ideas. Mind mapping activates your whole brain. It lets you develop a logical sequence and detailed organization of your material while encouraging imagination and spontaneity.

Mind mapping allows you to represent a tremendous amount of information in a relatively small space. You can have all your notes for a topic on one piece of paper, with your ideas arranged in a way that encourages you to see relationships between them. Mind mapping helps you see connections among things that may have seemed completely separate. It gives you a clear view of both the details and the big picture of your subject, thereby encouraging synvergent thinking.

Remembering your material also becomes much easier. Colors, images, and key words, three central ingredients of mind maps, are much more engaging to the brain than sentences. A well-made mind map is almost impossible to forget!

Perhaps the greatest advantage of mind mapping is that by nurturing your unique, individual self-expression it makes thinking, working, and problem solving a lot more fun.

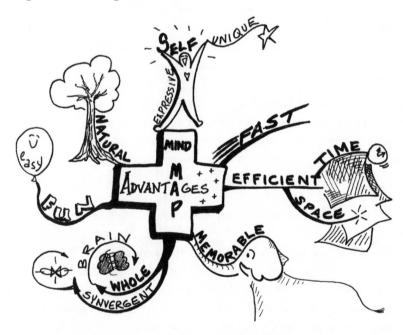

A mind map of the advantages of mind mapping.

Q: How does mind mapping train you to be a better thinker?

A: Mind mapping encourages you to use all of your brain's natural elements. By expressing your thoughts in a dimensional, colorful, pictorial, key, connected, free-flowing fashion, you nourish those elements of your thinking. The more you practice, the stronger these elements become. As the elements strengthen, your mind mapping improves, further nourishing the elements. Mind mapping develops the habit of creative, synvergent thinking through this virtuous cycle.

Mind mapping is also useful in liberating us from the preconceived ideas and prejudices that limit the freedom of our thinking and problem solving. Thinking skills pioneer Edward de Bono advocates an evolution away from what he calls our adversarial or argumentative approach to thinking. This approach is characterized by a tendency to use thinking as a means for defending our prejudices. De Bono points out that the argumentative approach to thinking was developed by medieval monks as a tool for discrediting heretics. Instead, he recommends "the *mapmaking* type of thinking in which the terrain is first explored and then noted. Then the possible routes are observed and finally a choice of route is made."

Mind mapping translates de Bono's mapmaking metaphor into a practical method that encourages a broad, exploratory, and more objective approach to thinking.

> *Make the map first.*
> *—Edward de Bono*

Applications of Mind Mapping

Mind mapping has many specific, practical, and immediately applicable uses. Let's explore some of the most popular and powerful applications.

LIFE MAPPING: SYNVERGENT GOAL SETTING

At some point in their careers, most citizens of the organizational world will spend days, if not weeks and months, writing vision, mission, and value statements. Yet very few people invest the same time and energy in defining their own goals. Many of us go through life without comprehensively considering what we want. If we do not choose consciously, our goals are set for us by others—bosses, parents, teachers, politicians, clergy, advertising, and the media, or by our automatic, repto-mammalian programming. Of course, we all think about our careers, relationships, and finances from time to time, but rarely, if ever, do we contemplate all our goals and how they fit together. As the saying goes, "If you don't know where you're going, any road will take you there."

Most books on self-help and self-development emphasize the importance of setting clear goals and for a good reason: people who write down their goals are more successful, happier, and wealthier than those who do not. Life mapping is a process of clarifying and integrating your personal life goals and values. Life mapping allows you to set down all your goals and values on one piece of paper so you can see how they fit together. By representing your major life goals in images and symbols, life mapping encourages you to *visualize* what you really want.

Begin by drawing a picture in the center of your paper that represents you. Make up your own logo or draw a symbol that resonates with your sense of who you are. From that central image, extend out and create a symbol for each of your life's major areas, such as values, purpose, family, career, finances, spirituality, health, hobbies, community service, friendships, travel, and learning.

These are a few sample life map central images.

Radiating from each of your main images, print the key words associated with each branch. Keep branching out until the general key concepts associated with each branch move into specifics. For example, in your branch on finances, you might have key words such as *security* or *abundance*. Continue until you define for yourself what these key words mean specifically (i.e., just how much money do you require?). Write the number down.

On a separate map, you may wish to explore strategies for creating the money you need. As you develop a strategy, check it against your other priorities as expressed in your life map.

After initially expressing your life goals and values, put the life map on the wall at home or in the office. Then contemplate the following questions: Do I have a clear set of goals? What are my priorities, values, and guiding principles? Are my goals ecological—do they all fit together and support one another? Are they in alignment with my principles and values, the things I really care about? Does my current mode of working, relating, learning, loving, relaxing, and budgeting time and money contribute to the achievement of my goals? What activities, people, and places bring out the best in me? What is my life's purpose? Am I traveling my own true path? Am I enjoying the journey? As you reflect on these questions you can refine and develop your life map further.

Many people avoid comprehensive consideration of their life goals, purpose, and values because they have a big "I can't" about living a life that reflects their ideals. Some ignore the issue because it means they might have to change their habits. Others have just been so busy cutting through the trees that they haven't taken the time to survey the forest.

One very bright student, a woman in her late thirties named Leah, was on the fast-track to the top of her Fortune 100 employer. In just seven years she'd risen from entry-level manager to senior director. There was only one problem. When Leah made her life map, she realized she wasn't fulfilled. Her first child had died at birth, and even though she successfully delivered a beautiful son a few years later she buried some of her grief in a constant drive for success and approval at work. She frequently felt stressed out and was short-tempered with her husband and young son. She had no time to pursue her ideal hobbies. Secretly, she yearned to have more children and the time to fully experience and nurture her family.

Leah's life map showed her surrounded by children, supporting her husband's career, and balancing the pursuit of her interests in music, fitness, and travel with a part-time consulting practice and community service work. Her life map also indicated that she would need substantial savings to create such a life.

She took her life map home and shared it with her husband, who agreed to support Leah's plan. Working together, they developed a savings and investment strategy to provide the necessary resources. Three years later, Leah gave birth to twin daughters. She left the corporate world to raise her children. She built a small consulting practice and became involved as a volunteer, counseling women who had lost their babies. And she saved enough to hire a part-time baby-sitter so she could take music lessons, join a health club, and travel with her husband on occasion. As she realigned her life to reflect her ideals, she became a much happier person and her relationship with her husband blossomed. Her support has helped him rise to the top of his profession.

Leah is now living a fulfilling and balanced life that reflects her values. And although she is busier than ever, stress does not seem to get the best of her anymore. Of course, none of this would have happened if Leah did not have the willingness to face her inconsistencies and the courage and resourcefulness to change. Life mapping served simply as a mirror for self-reflection and a catalyst for change.

As Leah realized, real success is living a life that reflects your values. When this harmony is absent, you experience a deep, gnawing inner tension, a vague sense that something is wrong. You become more vulnerable to stress. Stress is an unavoidable by-product of modern life. There is too much traffic, pollution, and information for anyone to ignore. But stress becomes distress when your life is out of alignment with your true goals and values. A sense of purpose is the best immunization against stress.

Of course, perfect alignment with one's highest ideals is elusive. Even saints have bad days. With self-acceptance and compassion as your point of departure, each day aim to take small steps toward achieving your goals and living your values. The journey of a thousand miles, according to the ancient Chinese proverb, begins with one step.

Make a habit of reflecting on your life map a few times each week, perhaps during brain breaks. Contemplating your life map on a regular basis will keep you focused on your true life path. Life mapping encourages you to take a synvergent perspective; viewing your clear focus on achieving specific goals in the context of a broader life vision.

Inspired by this process, one person I know had his life map photocopied in color, reduced, and inserted as the first page of his personal daily planning system. On the second page, he made a collage of photographs that represent his values and goals. A committed Christian, he carries a picture of Christ. A devoted family man, he treasures a photograph of his wife and children. His career goal is represented in the pose of himself poised behind a desk with the title Executive Vice President under his nameplate. Committed to abundance and to actualizing his ideal hobby of sailing, he included a picture of himself wearing a captain's hat, leaning against the side of a yacht. Each morning, as he reviews his plans for the day, he smiles as he visualizes what he cares about and wants to achieve.

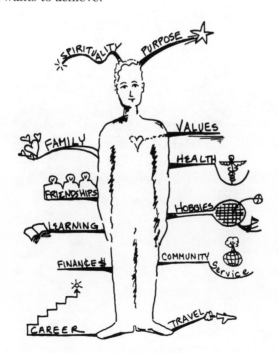

The beginning of a life map ...

LIFE MAPPING: LIVE YOUR PRIORITIES, PLAN YOUR TIME

Use your life map as a guide to living your priorities and managing your time. Translate your life map into a five-year goal map, and then into a one-year plan. At the beginning of each week, make a mind map of your weekly plan, color-coding each of your major life areas. This gives you instant visual feedback on your success in balancing your life's priorities. Contemplate the whole picture of your weekly plan. Is your week a balanced rainbow or a monochromatic blur? Have you planned enough time for nurturing your relationships, your health, your personal and spiritual development? As you survey your map ask how each activity you have planned supports the realization of your visions and values. Then, each day, make a mind map of your daily plan.

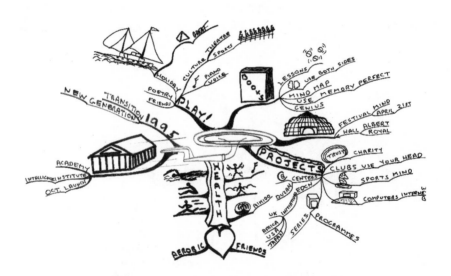

Tony Buzan's year-plan mind map for 1995. Tony chose the Starship Enterprise as his central image.

To translate your weekly plan into daily plans and your daily plans into effective actions requires distinguishing between different levels of priority and between priority and urgency. When you are running late for a meeting, your phone and fax are both ringing, and someone is knocking on your door it is hard to maintain the big picture. Everything seems to be happening too fast and it's easy to fall into the trap of forgetting priorities and responding to the most pressing elements in your environment.

Our repto-mammalian brain is programmed to give priority to immediate changes in our environment. Purposeful long-term thinking is a function of our newer, evolving mind and, without conscious commitment and reinforcement, is easily short-circuited.

The biggest time drain of daily life is investing energy in activities that are pressing but not "on purpose." Many meetings, phone calls, and other interruptions fall into this category. Of course, many pressing activities are also priorities: working on a major presentation with an imminent deadline, fixing a leak in your basement, or taking your child to the hospital after a nasty fall.

Many of our most significant priorities elude us, however, because they do not set off repto-mammalian alarm bells. We must discipline ourselves to use our higher awareness to invest appropriate time in non-pressing priorities, such as planning sessions, relationship building, and educational programs. Ironically, many harried managers protest that they are too busy and stressed to attend seminars on time and stress management. Appropriate time invested in nonpressing priorities progressively frees us from crisis management and is a key to living a balanced life.

You can make your days easier to manage by assessing your daily activities in a way that reflects the balance of pressure and priority. Consider your day in the light of this grid adapted from the work of Dr. Stephen Covey.

1. Pressing Priorities: crises, emergencies, and time-sensitive projects

2. Nonpressing Priorities: planning, cultivating relationships, creative thinking, education, and self-renewal

3. Pressing, Low Priority: many phone calls, meetings, reports, and interruptions

4. Nonpressing, Low Priority: reading junk mail, mindless television watching, and general trivia

Many of us spend too much time in squares 1, 3, and 4, and not enough in square 2. Obviously, effectiveness demands minimizing 3 and 4 and balancing 1 and 2.

At the end of each day, make a mind map of what you *actually* did. Color-code it by square (e.g., yellow for 1, blue for 2, orange for 3, and gray for 4), and compare it with your original "To Do" mind map. Adapt accordingly when making your next daily plan mind map.

As you review each day remember that time management is ultimately self-management. In addition to managing your tasks be sure to manage your perception of time. If you allow yourself to be run by pressing events, you lose your center and time seems short. If you remember to pause, breathe, and shift out of a reactive mode, your sense of time expands as you open yourself to contact with a timeless core of inner strength.

Your weekly and daily planning and self-management is the key to translating your life goals and values into reality. The small choices and decisions that you make every day determine the quality of your life.

VISIONCRAFT: WRITE STRATEGIC PLANS, MISSIONS, AND VALUE STATEMENTS

Visioncraft refers to the process of writing and creating a shared sense of meaning and responsibilty for visions, missions, strategies, ethics, values, and principles.

A **vision** is a cause, a crusade, a picture of a promised land that *inspires* you to arrive at work with enthusiasm. A **mission** guides *what* you do when you get there. A **strategy** is *how* you do it. A statement of **ethics, values,** or **principles** guides your *actions and relationships* with co-workers, clients, vendors, and other stakeholders.

Visioncrafting sets the tone for the success of any venture. To set the right tone, statements must be:

Juicy—inspiring, energizing, alive
Original—a unique expression of you, your company, or team
Succinct—every word packed with meaning
Inclusive—reflecting the concerns of all stakeholders
Positive—active, focused, and affirming
Memorable—everyone in the organization knows it by heart
Aligned—with universal principles and basic goodness
Integrated—into everyday behavior

MIND MAPPING VISIONCRAFT: BRIEF CASE HISTORIES

The following examples are offered to inspire and guide you in applying mind mapping visioncraft in your organization.

A recent two-day visioncrafting session for the customer services division of a major telecommunications company began with a day of training in mind mapping. (The company had recently written its overall vision, mission, and people principles through the visioncrafting process. The next step was to get each division of the company to craft its own vision in alignment with the big picture.) Although everyone seemed to be enjoying the training, a number of participants expressed anxiety. One person summed up the feeling by stating, "There's only one day left and we haven't gotten any real work done yet."

Day two began with an overview of the visioncrafting process and a presentation on the company's overall vision, mission, strategic priorities, and people principles. Preconference interviews with the team targeted four objectives: redefine the mission and strategy, create a more effective structure, improve communication between team members and with other teams in the company, and find new and better ways to serve customers.

With Mozart's *Eine Kleine Nachtmusic* playing in the background, each person was issued a piece of blank flip-chart paper and a set of colored pens and asked to draw a picture or symbol that represented the team in the center. On lines radiating out from the central image each person printed the key words: MISSION, STRUCTURE, COMMUNICATION, SERVICE.

Participants then *free-associated* on these topics, expressing their thoughts in key words (printed, one per line) and pictures. After forty-five minutes, a ten-minute break, and fifteen more minutes for individual mind mapping (the break provides an opportunity for "incubation" that often results in an Aha!), the team divided into groups of four.

Each group member took five minutes for a show-and-tell presentation of their mind map. As they expressed their ideas the others listened carefully. The presentations were followed by twenty minutes of group discussion, with an emphasis on finding the synergy of ideas.

After sharing their views on all four objectives, team members were assigned to task forces focusing on one of the key objectives. Again, they began with forty-five minutes of individual mind mapping, followed by a show-and-tell and then a synergy focused discussion.

Each group then created a consensus mind map of their views and recommendations to present to the larger team. Key points of each presentation were recorded on a master mind map. When the presentations were complete, the floor was opened for discussion with a focus on the synergy of ideas and practical applications.

The mission group translated their mind map into a more traditional document that met with unanimous approval. The structure group suggested three key changes; the vice president agreed to implement two of them on the spot and agreed to study the third and make a decision within two weeks. The communications group recommended a series of initiatives, adopted by acclamation, to make the company's people principles come to life. The service group inspired the entire team by devising a strategy to make the whole company more customer-focused and by developing new approaches to anticipating needs and improving customer relationships. This inspired one of the groups' directors to comment:

> The people in this division feel a strong commitment to our work though most of us haven't worked together before. Despite some skepticism, the mind mapping process allowed us to come together as a team in an unprecedented way. In just two days we understood how similar our concerns are. Building on individual strengths and experience, from the newest intern to our vice president, we began to see how our separate visions can come together into a unifying whole that helps each of us contribute to our company's success.

Mind mapping is also an invaluable tool for creating a statement of organizational values and people principles. Many organizations function effectively without explicitly defining what they value, but when changes occur, they are forced to take a fresh look at themselves.

In 1991, the organizational culture at a major corporate pension fund was a cross between the relatively benign, entitlement-oriented bureaucracy, typical of the corporation, and the numbers-oriented "me-first" culture of Wall Street. The fund was divided into an investment services group, and the more prestigious investment professionals. The stratification of the organization was expressed by placing "services" people on the tenth floor and "professionals" on the eleventh. At the bottom of the totem pole, the secretarial staff was treated as "gofers."

The fund's newly appointed director initiated a process to redefine the organization's mission and strategic plan. The plan called for improved communications with clients to anticipate opportunities and meet changing needs. It stressed the importance of a disciplined, value-based approach to investing combined with teamwork and creative thinking to "add value" for the client.

Although the new director sought broad participation in writing the plan, there were a number of cultural obstacles to its fulfillment. Besides the obvious tensions arising from stratification, other impediments existed. The investment professionals judged their success or failure purely by performance numbers. Teamwork had no place in their world view. Moreover, many people perceived the new emphasis on listening to the customer and giving high-powered presentations as a distraction from their "real" jobs. The idea of doing rigorous, high-quality investment work *and* effectively communicating with the client was new and threatening.

The task of changing the culture started from the bottom up, beginning with a retreat for the secretaries, that focused on building pride, empowerment, and effectiveness. The secretaries renamed themselves "office coordinators" (OCs) and decided that they could more effectively meet the organization's needs if they worked as a support team and reported to a team leader, instead of the traditional boss/secretary system. Working with mind maps, they wrote a mission statement and strategic initiatives. They even designed their own logo.

The project with the OCs was just the beginning. Tenth- and eleventh-floor people formed new, integrated work teams and organized a Values Task Force. This group interviewed everyone in the organization, asking questions designed to unearth "cultural" strengths and weaknesses and suggest a path forward. After the interviews were complete, a meeting of the task force was held (task force meetings were open to all) to compare findings and begin constructing a value statement.

As participants reported their findings, they were noted on a mind map at the front of the room. During the first four hours of the meeting, the group poured out frustrations and angst. Pandora's box had been opened and repressed demons were vented with vengeance. The meeting was extraordinary in its intensity of emotion and in the universality of themes discovered by the group. One person after another complained about a lack of leadership, a dearth of development opportunities, poor communication, and a shortage of trust and mutual respect. Although the issue of differing compensation levels was mentioned by everyone, much more energy was focused on a universal sense of inadequate recognition. People didn't feel valued and appreciated.

The tone of the reports suggested that "they" were responsible for all this. The first breakthrough came after lunch when the group was asked: "How many of you can honestly say that you have given adequate recognition to the people you work with in the past week?" All who felt that they had done so were asked to stand. Everyone remained seated. Then someone exclaimed, "These are our problems. We created them and we've got to solve them!"

The group contemplated the "problem map" made in the morning session. Together, they experienced a revelation—the problems mapped *were* their values! The emotion that had accompanied their expression was a sign of just how much everyone really cared about these things.

As the leader of the task force commented, "The mind mapping process acted as a mirror of truth, reflecting our values and encouraging our empowerment." Using the original mind map as a guide, the task force wrote their value statement, which was ultimately signed and endorsed by the entire organization.

Of course, writing a value statement doesn't magically create a utopian culture, but it sets the stage for a more humane, intelligent, and effective workplace.

TREND MAPPING

Rather than sit around waiting for change to conk them on the head, savvy people aim to anticipate trends. They subscribe to "trend letters" from forecasting firms, think tanks, and Wall Street advisers. They seek an edge by consulting books such as Naisbitt's *Megatrends* and Toffler's *Powershift*. In addition to these worthy pursuits, try a more assertive option. Use mind mapping to track trends yourself.

In his bestseller *Trend Tracking,* Gerald Celente not only offers insights into the future, he also provides guidance on how you can predict it. Celente suggests that all you need to begin is an open, inquisitive mind and a willingness to practice. He advocates daily, critical reading of newspapers such as *USA Today, The New York Times, The Wall Street Journal,* and other national and international publications. As you learn to separate real news from junk news and trends from fads, you can record and integrate the key data on mind maps, constructing your own pictures of the future.

Celente warns that many would-be forecasters do excellent analysis but draw inaccurate conclusions because they look at the world from the narrowed perspective of their discipline. He points out that economists, for example, are frequently wrong because they make predictions using only economic data, ignoring social, political, and other information. Celente emphasizes that "the real world is more complex than their quantitative models, however elegant."

Celente emphasizes that *the best prognosticators are distinguished by their ability to make connections between seemingly unrelated fields.* Mind mapping makes it easier to see the world synvergently, making new connections and constructing a picture of the future. You can launch your trend-mapping endeavors by trying this "big picture" exercise.

Make mind maps on the changes you have observed in your lifetime in each of the following areas: education, environment, technology, social, political, economic, spiritual. After you complete all seven maps, color-code the seven most important changes on each one. Next, draw a picture of the globe in the center of a large sheet of paper and make main branches corresponding to your original mind map topics—education, environment, technology, and so on.

Print key words representing the significant changes you have identified on lines radiating from the appropriate branch. Survey the big picture. What are the elements that appear on more than one branch? Look for patterns, relationships, anomalies. Use arrows, colors, and codes to represent the connections you make.

Using your big picture as a point of departure, you can mind map your prognostications for the fields that you find most compelling. Celente tracks everything from advertising and biotechnology to waste disposal and zoning.

Chaos is order without predictability.
—*T. J. Cartwright, physicist*

SELF-ANALYSIS AND INSIGHT

Do you ever have days when you're in a bad mood but don't quite know why? Or perhaps, like most people, you occasionally feel anxious or troubled by some nagging doubt or feeling of anxiety.

Take a large sheet of blank paper and draw a picture in the center that represents your feelings. Obviously, this drawing will tend toward abstract art. Art therapists use this exercise to help their clients get more in touch with themselves. They know that pictures and colors add depth and dimension to the voice of our emotions.

After you create a central image, use it as the home base for a mind map. Let your associations flow freely, printing key words on connected lines. As different shades of feeling arise, give them color and form on your mind map. This process is cathartic and it often yields a deeper understanding of what troubles you. Although not a panacea, it does help clarify things and frequently prompts significant insights.

An amusing example of the efficacy of this approach occurred during a seminar in Washington, D.C. The participants were mostly human resource and training directors. Among them was a woman known as the "queen of local pop psychology." Clothed in a flowing red dress, a bright red carnation in her big auburn hair, this Southern belle was a formidable character.

I didn't need to be a body language expert to recognize the distress signals from her angular posture and sullen expression. Obviously, something bothered her. When I took her aside during the mind mapping exercise and asked if I could help, she sighed and announced, "I *hate* mind mappin'!"

I told her to forget about the exercise that the rest of the class was doing, and asked if instead she would be willing to do a special mind map on her feelings about mind mapping. Fortunately, the idea struck a chord. She made one of the most striking mind maps I've ever seen.

First she drew a purple tunnel crawling with green spiders swirling in a black vortex. Then she scrawled key words like *fear, confusion, anxiety*. Almost immediately, her mood improved as her posture and expression expanded. When I asked for a progress report, she beamed, "I *love* mind mappin'." It was just her "resistance" getting in the way, she explained. So, when y'all are feelin' your resistance, try mapping it out!

PLAN A VACATION

Plan your next vacation using a mind map. If you are vacationing with others, such as your family, ask each person to make a mind map of what he or she would like to do. Then combine them into one family vacation mind map. Look for common interests and ways to fulfill them. This process encourages family team building while making the process of planning a lot more fun.

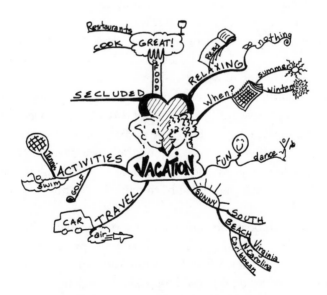

Plan your next vacation with a mind map.

PLAN PARTIES AND SOCIAL EVENTS

One of my clients used a mind map to plan a dinner party. She drew stick figures of the guests with key words representing their interests and distinguishing characteristics. She made simple illustrations of the menu items and wines she planned to serve. In addition to helping her generate and organize all the elements for the party, the mind map proved so aesthetically pleasing that she made color copies and used them as place mats!

SUPER STUDY SKILLS

In 1993, as a senior at North Miami High School in Florida, Lana Israel won first place in the behavioral and social sciences division of the 44th International Science and Engineering Fair. She also won the Glenn T. Seaborg Nobel Prize Visit Award given to the overall winner, chosen from an initial pool of over one million students. In addition, Lana received special awards from the U.S. Army, Air Force, Federal Aviation Administration, and the American Psychological Association. Lana, now a student at Harvard, was also the first *child* ever invited to speak at the World Conference of Teachers of Gifted and Talented Students. Apple Computer President John Sculley observed that "Lana will change the world!"

What is the secret of Lana'a extraordinary success? In her own words:

> In the seven years that I've been mind mapping, my whole approach to studying has undergone a massive transformation. Mind mapping has turned studying into a quick, exciting, and enjoyable learning process, as opposed to a seemingly endless period of drudgery and boredom. In addition to dramatically reducing the amount of time I spend studying, mind mapping has allowed me to turn tomes of facts, figures, and formulas into manageable and comprehensive units of information. Yet, it is perhaps the intangible benefits of mind mapping that are most significant. For mind mapping has enabled students around the world, myself included, to realize the astonishing potential we all possess—the power of the human brain.

Knowledge is power and, in the information age, knowledge is more powerful than ever. Students of all ages can make study faster, easier, and more fun by applying mind mapping. Mind mapping lets you integrate and remember material from books and lectures in a brain-friendly fashion. When studying books or other written material, try the following approach adapted from Tony Buzan's Organic Study Method:

Create a **brain-nourishing environment.** Access an **"I can" attitude.** Imagine your thirty billion brain cells primed to absorb, learn, and remember. **Browse** through your study material, assessing its organization and the accessibility of key information. Is the table of contents clear and well organized? Are there study questions at the end of each chapter? Is the text illustrated? Are there any summary, conclusion, or review sections?

Set a **specific time** for your study session and target a **specific amount** of material (e.g., sixty pages of history text and thirty pages of science in three hours).

Do a three- to five-minute **brain-burst mind map** on your current knowledge of the subject. This will warm up your brain, tuning your associative process to the right knowledge-reception frequency.

Note your objectives. What, specifically, do you want to learn? By approaching books with an active objective in mind, you learn faster and more effectively. In a classic study, two groups of students were asked to study the same book. The first group was told that they were responsible for the whole book. The second group was given the objective of discerning the three major themes. When tested, the three themes group did better on all aspects of the exam, including the questions that were unrelated to the three themes. By setting specific objectives you get more from all your study.

Overview your text. Read the table of contents, introduction, chapter summaries, questions, review, or conclusion sections first. Scour the text for key information related to your objectives and note it on a mind map.

This overview phase of the study process is very powerful. During a workshop on study skills attended by 150 students and teachers at Paint Branch High School in Maryland, a young man informed me, "I hate books and I hate studying." His teacher had warned me that he was a delinquent who probably would not cooperate in the study exercise. I told the youngster that he didn't have to study and asked him if he would do me a favor and try making a mind map of the table of contents and chapter summaries of the text in question. He agreed. When the study session ended, I divided the class into small groups, mixing students and teachers, and asked each group member to use their mind map to give a five-minute book report presentation. The "delinquent" gave a presentation that his teacher described as "cogent, brilliant, and unbelievable!"

Preview the book by chapter. Key information often is packed into the beginning and end of each chapter. Read these sections next, noting key points on your mind map.

After forty to sixty minutes, take a **brain break.** Pause for five or ten minutes. Listen to your favorite music, do some stretching exercises, juggle, or meditate. Then return to your work refreshed, confident that your mind is busy assimilating the material you have studied.

Now read the rest of the book, focusing on the material most relevant to your objectives. If something is irrelevant, redundant, or already familiar, skip it and move on to the "meat." Record morsels of knowledge on your mind map.

Integrate and organize your mind map. Look for relationships between the branches. Do new themes or insights emerge as you scan the whole picture? You may wish to make a new mind map, reordering your main branches to express your evolving understanding.

As soon as possible, **teach someone** what you have just learned. If you can't find an interested audience, teach your teddy bear or pillow. The important thing is to practice expressing what you have learned. As you do, you gain a deeper understanding of what you know as well as a clearer idea of where you need further study. The practice of expressing your knowledge orients you toward mastery.

In addition to its potency in noting reading material, mind mapping can be used to improve your ability to **take notes from meetings, lectures, and seminars.** Mind mapping originated as a note-taking tool, designed to help students capture the essence of lectures with minimal effort and maximum return. Mind mapping also enhances your ability to think critically about the value of a lecture. A senior partner in a Wall Street investment firm summed up these applications of mind mapping in a letter: "First, I must admit that I came to the bat-tle as a bit of a skeptic . . . but two or three things have happened that have absolutely convinced me of the efficacy of mind mapping. To begin, I have found that I can take notes using this technique with a great deal more ease than I used to be able to, and more important, I can go back and look at these and remember what was said and what I thought at the time. Further, an unexpected but most important benefit has come from this, to wit, if someone is talking nonsense you find out immediately as it is impossible to map his thoughts. You sim-ply end up with an idea in the middle and a great many individual twigs coming off it but no real branches."

You can use mind mapping to prepare for exams by applying the **mind map memory method.** Take mind map notes from books and lectures and combine them into a master test-preparation mind map. Then put your master mind map aside and re-create it on a new sheet of paper. Check your re-created mind map against the original and fill in anything you may have left out. Do this until you can perfectly re-create your mind map from memory. Next, close your eyes and prac-tice visualizing your mind map in your mind's eye. Do this until you can see a vivid picture of all your notes. Now, walk into your exam with all your notes, legally!

On essay exams, if permissible, mind map the answers in the mar-gins of the exam paper or on scrap paper. These mind maps will make it much easier to generate and organize your answers.

EFFECTIVE TRAINING PROGRAMS

When I first led seminars in the corporate world in the late 1970s and early 1980s, I found that although individuals responded enthusiasti-cally, the organization often viewed training sessions as an entertain-ing diversion, an opportunity to think some new thoughts before returning to "business as usual." I once offered some suggestions to the training manager of a Fortune 500 company on how to apply creative thinking and communication skills in the workplace. He responded— I am not making this up—"Oh, we don't need to apply anything, we just need to run people through a certain number of hours of training."

Now, there is a new emphasis on training as an integral tool in creating a "learning organization." Companies are increasingly desperate to *apply* the lessons of training. Organizations invest billions in training their people in everything from accounting and computers to teamwork and quality. People go off for a few days to a hotel or conference center to learn a new skill or approach to business. Then they return to the workplace and are greeted by a major traffic jam on their personal information superhighway: overflowing piles of paper, a backlog of e-mail, and seventeen voice-mail messages. It should come as no surprise that most people forget 80 percent of what they learn on these programs in the first twenty-four hours; the remaining 20 percent atrophies over the next six months.

The first step in creating a learning organization is to take learning and training seriously and to apply synvergent thinking in the design and delivery of a training curriculum. When mind mapping is used to scope out the goals, content, and processes of a training curriculum, it is much more likely that the result will reflect a systems awareness. Companies such as Motorola, for example, have transformed their cultures and the quality of their products by making a profound commitment to comprehensive, integrated training. But, regardless of the brilliance of a training plan, its usefulness is limited by the extent to which people actually remember what they have learned!

Mind mapping offers a simple, powerful approach to remembering, integrating, and applying the learning from training programs. Try the following after your next training session: at the end of the session participants make a comprehensive mind map of everything they have learned. Then, working in groups of three to five, each person guides colleagues on a tour of their mind map, emphasizing the most significant elements of the new learning and plans for applying it. Within twenty-four hours of the end of the program each participant practices the mind map memory method, re-creating their mind map from memory. Then, sometime during the first week after the course, participants use their mind maps to teach what they learned to someone who did not attend.

One week after the end of the session, each participant spends thirty minutes with a fellow graduate re-creating the material and coaching each other on its application. This exercise is repeated one month and then six months later. These few hours of follow-up make a dramatic difference; people actually remember and apply much more of what they learn. To strengthen application further, the first hour of subsequent training programs is devoted to re-creating, in mind map form, the learning from previous programs. So every program builds on its predecessors, reinforcing and synergizing a living body of knowledge.

Like the number of synaptic patterns your brain can create, the number of possible uses for mind maps is virtually infinite. In addition to the above-mentioned examples, mind mapping is also useful for writing books, articles and reports, tracking criminal investigations, career planning, decision making, delivering performance reviews, and budgeting.

Two other uses of mind mapping are so potent and far-ranging that I have woven them into the fabric of separate chapters. Mind mapping is a catalyst for the process of creative problem solving—the subject of Chapter 3—and a powerful tool for improving communication and presentation skills, the subject of Chapters 4 and 5.

And there is one use of mind mapping that is part of all others. The regular practice of mind mapping awakens your latent powers of synvergent intelligence, training you to be a fast, focused, flexible thinker.

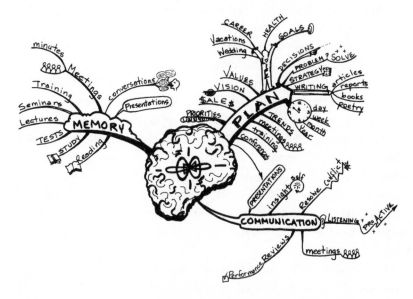

A mind map of the applications of mind mapping.

Wake Up Your Brain!

When I was in the ninth grade my teacher offered me the classic line—"You'll never amount to anything!" I was, to say the least, disenchanted with school. I particularly disliked writing term papers and reports on subjects that seemed to have no relevance to my life. This attitude was reflected in my grades, which were just above failing. In tenth grade, realizing that the price of resisting school was greater than the effort it would take to succeed, I resolved to improve. I started to do homework, study for tests, and tell my teachers more of what they wanted to hear. It worked. I became an honor student and was accepted by the university of my choice.

In college, it soon became apparent that the academic game was the same, it was just to be played with bigger words linked by *therefores* and *indeeds*. I graduated with honors in three years with a double major in psychology and philosophy, knowing something very valuable. *I knew that I knew nothing of real value.*

Seeking something more authentic, I found a progressive university that allowed me to work independently on a self-designed master's degree program in psycho-physical reeducation. The graduation requirements included attending a series of colloquia, writing quarterly progress reports, and completing a thesis of at least one hundred pages. Although I was pursuing an area of passionate interest and was encouraged to express my own ideas, when it came time to write my thesis, I was stuck. I felt uncomfortable with the ambiguity that writing brings . . . facing the unknown in the form of a blank page. When I tried to outline my ideas, I wasted a lot of time "waiting for idea roman numeral one." It was a terribly frustrating process.

Then I learned mind mapping from Tony Buzan. I drew a picture in the center of a big sheet of paper that represented the topic of my thesis. I began free-associating, linking key words with connected lines. My mind exploded with ideas. Freed from the compulsion to organize prematurely, my ability to enter into unknown territory expanded dramatically. Anxiety transformed into enthusiasm. I covered the walls of my apartment with mind maps. I consolidated these into a "master mind map," organized by main branches, which emerged almost effortlessly. These main branches became the chapters of my thesis, which, guided by my mind maps, I wrote in longhand.

When I was awarded my master's degree, the chairman of the thesis committee stated that in his entire academic career he had never seen such an improvement in a student's writing. As he put it, "You appear to have discovered your own true voice." Indeed!

All my books, including this one, were written from mind maps. I make mind maps the same way I did while working on my thesis. But now, instead of laborious longhand, I use a dictation machine and computer to write the book from the mind map. In addition to applying mind mapping in my writing, I use it to develop and plan all my speeches and seminars, to set goals and solve problems in my business and personal life, and to plan vacations, parties, and weekly and daily schedules. My wife and I even used it to plan our wedding.

Mind mapping transforms talk about unlimited human potential into reality. In 1980, Tony Buzan and I taught mind mapping to a group of 500 schoolchildren in Soweto, South Africa. A twelve-year-old boy named Hezekiel wrote afterward: "Before your course I did not think I was very smart. Now I know I have a wonderful brain. Now my school is much easier." After a course in Japan, a manager wrote, "Thank you very much for finally you wake up my brain!"

More than any of its specific applications, the greatest power of mind mapping comes from the effect its regular practice has on your thinking. It won't make you smarter—just as smart as you really are, which is smarter than you think. Use it to wake up your brain, to unleash your synvergent powers, to discover your true voice.

Chapter 3

— ⊰※⊱ —

Problems? Synvergent Solutions!

Introduction: In Your Right Mind

Life is an exercise in creative problem solving. Our minds are geared first to solve problems of survival—to guide us to food ("Where's the beef?"), shelter ("Home, on the Range"), and procreative possibilities ("Help me, Rhonda").

As basic needs are met, our attention shifts to questions of status ("We're #1"), esteem ("I Gotta Be Me"), and friendship ("A friend in need is a friend indeed"). Then, ultimately we seek truth ("Seek and ye shall find"), beauty ("Beauty is truth, truth beauty"), and love ("There is a light that shines beyond all things on earth, beyond the highest, the very highest heavens. This is the light that shines in your heart").

Whatever the level of your problems, you can solve them more effectively by deepening your understanding of the nature of the mind. In 1890, William James offered these challenging thoughts on the nature of mind: "Our normal waking consciousness . . . is but one special type of consciousness, whilst all about it, parted from it by the flimsiest of screens there lie potential forms of consciousness entirely different. We may go through life without suspecting their existence; but apply the requisite stimulus, and at a touch they are there in all their completeness, definite types of mentality which probably somewhere have their field of application and adaptation." James added: "No account of the universe in its totality can be final, which leaves these other forms of consciousness quite disregarded. How to regard them is the question—for they may determine attitudes though they cannot furnish formulas, and open a region though they fail to give a map."

Brain scientists have confirmed that our minds are made up of different types of mentality. Although most of us hold the conviction that our normal rational mind is a unified whole, recent research suggests that this belief is an illusion. Our minds are a compilation of myriad automated routines—subject, but rarely subjected, to the influence of our consciousness.

We have many minds and function best when we find the right mind for a given task. To discover our mind's appropriate fields of application and adaptation, consciousness must furnish formulas and give a map.

Of course it is possible to redirect the mind consciously, playing different thinking roles appropriate to different phases of the problem-solving process. But, like learning to juggle or play chess, this ability has to be cultivated. We know, for example, that left-brainers prefer to look at problems from an analytical perspective, while righties prefer a more imaginative approach. Pessimists are often uncomfortable in problem-solving situations unless they play the role of devil's advocate, looking for the downside of every proposition, while optimists look on the bright side and may ignore pitfalls.

Similarly, some people are happy asking challenging questions and initiating new endeavors, while others enjoy assessing the value of ideas and driving projects to completion. Each of us, however, has the capacity to think and act in all of these ways. Right-brainers can "play the role" of detail-oriented, analysts. Just as ex-prosecutors make great defense attorneys, devil's advocates can effectively represent angels and initiators can learn the strategies and skills of finishers and vice versa.

The approach presented in this chapter is based on the idea that each of us is capable of accessing different aspects of mind appropriate to different parts of the problem-solving process. We can improve our effectiveness by nurturing different styles of thinking beyond our habitual dominant ways. The synvergent formulas furnished in this chapter offer a map that guides you to take advantage of your own internal diversity. You can apply these strategies to create a superpowered, personal brainstorming resource and to develop your ability as a leader, building high-performance problem-solving groups such as work teams, community organizations, and your family.

THE FIVE PHASES OF CREATIVE PROBLEM SOLVING

The problem-solving or solution-finding process has five phases that pulse between an emphasis on focused/convergent and diffuse/divergent modes of thinking.

Preparation: Define your problem or question, question preconceptions, conduct research, and commit to the process.

Generation: Brainstorm; move beyond habitual pathways of thought.

Incubation: Allow your subattentional intelligence to suggest solutions; sleep on it.

Evaluation: Analyze and evaluate proposed solutions; make decisions.

Implementation: Plan for action; act.

Each of these phases calls for different "minds" and corresponding thinking roles. As you expand your understanding of the phases, you enhance your freedom to choose the right mind and most effective roles for your situation. Let's explore the phases in depth.

Preparation: The Jeopardy! Effect

What is problem solving and how does it begin? The verb *solve* comes from the root *solvere*, which means "to loosen, release, or set free." The word *problem* comes from the roots *pro*, meaning "forward" and *ballein*, meaning to "throw or drive." *Webster's* defines a problem as, "a question proposed for solution or consideration." So, problem solving is the process of proposing and considering questions in a way that throws or drives us forward toward greater freedom.

The process of problem solving begins with understanding and defining the problem. Frequently, as in the game show *Jeopardy!*, the appropriate question provides a solution. In many problem-solving sessions, success requires replacing or reframing the initial question. The essence of the preparation phase is to find the most useful questions to inspire your creative powers, and then to commit to the process of successfully exploring, managing, or solving them.

> *You can tell whether a man is clever by his answers. You can tell whether a man is wise by his questions.*
> —*Naguib Mahfouz, Nobel Prize winner*

Of course, some problems are simple and clearly defined, such as: Who is buried in Grant's tomb?* or "What is seven times seven? These questions have just one answer. In a normal universe, given the rules of arithmetic, seven times seven will always equal forty-nine. Much of our schooling focuses on solving these kinds of problems. We are trained to ask, "What is the right answer?"

More complex problems have many possible solutions. Instead of

---

*Of course, one could argue that the casket and soil surronding Grant's body contain decomposed remnants of numerous life forms, probably including some prehistoric human relatives, but, for everyday practical purposes the answer is, Grant.

asking What's the right answer? it is more constructive to ask, Is this the right question? and What are some possible solutions or paths forward?

One of the classic questions businesspeople ask is, "How can we increase sales?" There are myriad possible approaches: have a sale, advertise, offer rebates or frequent-buyer awards, stay open twenty-four hours, give better service, improve the product, beef-up the sales force, get an 800 number, provide better sales training, offer incentives to the sales team, and on and on.

Of course, it's possible to increase sales and lose money. Like the vacuum cleaner company in England that offered free international airline tickets to customers who purchased a new vacuum. The tickets were more expensive than the vacuums and they sold *lots* of vacuums. It cost them millions.

Frequently individuals and organizations make the mistake of framing their questions and problems in a vacuum. Questions about sales are framed without reference to profits. Questions about profits are framed without reference to people. This way of framing problems is based on a compartmentalized either/or worldview. Instead, define the details of your questions synvergently, in a way that reflects the whole picture.

Many of the problems we deal with in organizational and personal life are complex, and initially, rather vague, such as How can we build teamwork? or How can I be happy? These problems can be defined and framed in a wide variety of ways, and the framing will dramatically influence your solution finding.

The author of *Polarity Management*, Dr. Barry Johnson, emphasizes that linear thinkers tend to frame these challenges as a movement toward one element (the solution, i.e., teamwork or happiness) and away from the other (the problem, i.e., individuality and unhappiness). But, these complex issues are best understood as pairs of interdependent opposites. If, for example, individuals do not feel recognized for their unique contributions, teamwork is unlikely. If one seeks happiness directly, unhappiness is always around the corner.

Psychologist Mark Brown offers the example of a question redefinition that resulted in a major transformation of human societies. Nomadic societies were based on the question, How do we get to water? They became agrarian and stable cultures, Brown says, when they began asking, How do we get the water to come to us?

How can you develop your problem definition skills so that solutions will start to come to you?

Begin by cultivating your ability to play the role of an insatiably curious child. Often the most useful questions are the simple, naive questions that sophisticated people are prone to overlook. Ask awkward questions like: Why is the emperor naked? Why is this a problem? Is this the real problem? Why have we always done it this way?

The classic reporter's questions—what? where? when? who? how? why?—help you get right to the heart of the matter. Think of a problem that you are concerned with in your professional or personal life, and ask:

What
. . . is the problem?

. . . are the underlying issues?

. . . can it be compared to or what metaphors can I use to illuminate it? (For example, the inventor of the pull-tab top for aluminum cans was inspired by asking, "What, in nature, opens easily?" A picture of a banana popped into his mind, leading him to ask, "How can the design of the banana serve as a model for the task at hand?")

. . . will happen if I ignore it?

. . . problems may be caused by solving this problem?

. . . polarities or oppositional elements are inherent within it?

When
. . . did it start?

. . . does it happen?

. . . doesn't it happen?

. . . will the consequences of it be felt?

Who
. . . cares about it?

. . . is affected by it?

. . . created it?

. . . perpetuates it?

. . . can help solve it?

Where
. . . does it happen?
. . . did it begin?
. . . haven't I looked?
. . . else has this happened?
Why
. ? . is it important?
. . . did it start?
. . . does it continue?
How
. . . does it happen?
. . . can I look at it differently?
. . . can it be changed?
. . . does my investment in solving this problem look in light of my
vision and values?
. . . will I know that it has been solved?

Although there are no set rules for framing questions, it is generally
useful to seek a balance between broad generalization and overspe-
cialization between flexibility and focus. A well-framed question is
provocative, energizing, and inspiring. Look at the details of your problem in the context of the big picture. Seek alternate ways to frame your
question, look for interdependent opposites, and remember that there
may be more than one right answer.

MIND SET: LOOKING FOR MONKEYS

The "frame" for problems is important because it organizes your sense
of purpose, and your purposes tend to determine your perceptions.
Perception follows purpose. For example, if you decide to buy a four-
wheel-drive vehicle, and ask yourself, "What's the best four-wheel-
drive for me?" then you can be sure that next time you are out on the
road or walking through a parking lot, you will notice Explorers, Jeeps,
and Range Rovers in record numbers. You will notice advertisements
and articles in magazines and newspapers related to four-wheelers
that you probably would have ignored before you set your mind on
four-wheel drive.

At a seminar one day, someone used the word *armamentarium.* Two days later, a fellow student exclaimed: "Until the other day, when you mentioned 'armamentarium,' I had never heard the word, so I looked it up. Since then, I've encountered it twice from different sources."

Field biologist Anna Novak spends much of her time observing primates in Panamanian jungles. She mentioned to our mutual friend, author Gerald Celente, that although the jungle was full of monkeys, she never saw any snakes. Then one day she invited a colleague who specialized in snakes to join her foray into the forest. Within moments, a snake appeared, and then another, and another. In the end, they spotted over fifty snakes! As Celente describes it: "Anna was puzzled. She asked her colleague why she hadn't seen them before. He said because she was looking for monkeys."

The phenomenon of seeing what we expect or want to see is called "mental set." It functions all the time, consciously or unconsciously. A limited, unconscious mental set retards our solution-finding ability.

As Abraham Maslow stated, "People who are only good with a hammer see every problem as a nail." Follow Maslow's thinking with this warning: If the man who only has a hammer treats everything as a nail, watch out for the man who only has a screwdriver.

Mark McCormack, the founder of the International Management Group and author of *What They Don't Teach You at Harvard Business School,* describes the limiting mental set that is often created by formal business training: "A master's in business can sometimes block an ability to master experience. Many of the early MBAs we hired were either congenitally naive or victims of their business training. The result was a kind of real-life learning disability—a failure to read people properly or to size up situations and an uncanny knack for forming the wrong perceptions."

Bennett Goodspeed, cofounder of Inferential Focus and author of *The Tao Jones Averages,* shared similar sentiments. He once said: "If Thomas Edison had an MBA, he would have tried to invent a bigger candle!"

MBA or not, one of the critical keys to creative problem solving is learning to expand your mind-set by cultivating an open, questing state of mind. Leonardo da Vinci offers a beautiful illustration of this productive mind-set:

I roamed the countryside searching for answers to things I did not understand. Why shells existed on the tops of mountains along with the imprints of coral and plants and seaweed usually found in the sea. Why the thunder lasts a longer time than that which causes it, and why immediately on its creation the lightning becomes visible to the eye while thunder requires time to travel. How the various circles of water form around the spot which has been struck by a stone, and why a bird sustains itself in the air. These questions and other strange phenomena engage my thought throughout my life.

Great minds ask great questions. The questions that "engage our thought" on a daily basis reflect our life purpose and influence the quality of our lives. By cultivating a da Vinci-like, open, questing frame of mind, we broaden our universe and improve our ability to travel through it.

When Richard Feynman (57) was a youngster his mother asked the future Nobel Prize winner the same question every evening at the dinner table: "What did you ask at school today, Richard?"

KNOW YOUR FEELINGS

Feelings play an intrinsic role in the search for solutions. Intuition, hunches, and gut feelings can be our most valuable allies. But feelings can also lead us to be biased and blind to truth. Unmonitored, emotions determine our mental sets, setting the agenda for our perception and thinking.

Ultimately our actions are determined by emotion. We choose a particular course because, in the final analysis, it feels right. The key question is: When does our emotional judgment serve us best? Should we use it at the beginning, allowing our feelings to determine our perceptions and thoughts? Or should we try to allow our perception and thinking to operate objectively first, then applying gut feeling to the assembled data to make our decision?

Clearly, to make the most of your mind, it's best to suspend emotion until the point of decision. So, an essential part of the preparation phase is separating feelings from perception. To do this, we must first know what our feelings are. Ask yourself: "How do I feel about this problem?" "What are my real feelings about it?" "Do I have any prejudices, fears, or limiting mental sets that prevent me from assessing this situation accurately?"

CONDUCT RESEARCH: A NEW SPIN

Success favors the prepared mind.
—*Louis Pasteur*

One of the great misconceptions about creative thinking is that it appears out of nowhere. This is false. Creativity is the result of a new combination of existing elements. Studies of highly creative individuals reveal that they nurture their creativity through a continuous quest for knowledge. Herman Melville, for example, immersed himself in the study of whales and whaling prior to writing *Moby Dick*.

Memory is a storehouse for the ingredients of the creative problem-solving process. As we learned in Chapter 2, the more you know the more you can know. And, the more you know the more your capacity for creativity expands.

To frame a question or problem effectively, it is often necessary to gather and deposit in memory more information, to conduct research. Data, information, facts, impressions, knowledge, understanding, associations, statistics, concepts, and theories form the base ingredients for any creative recipe.

Some of the most useful questions to ask in conducting your research are: What information do I need to solve this? Where is it available? Who has experience with this sort of problem? Has someone already solved this?

Most solutions and innovations involve small adaptations of previous discoveries. You will frequently find that rather than reinvent the wheel, all you need to do is give it a new spin.

A few weeks ago I was looking for my watch. I thought it must be somewhere in my study, so I decided to clean and organize the whole room while searching. I found the watch and in the process found a book I thought I had lost and a five-dollar bill!

If you approach your research with an open, questing mind, you may find what you are looking for . . . and more.

Effective researchers cultivate objectivity. If you are in touch with your feelings, you can look at your problem or a question objectively. Much of what passes for objectivity is a dangerous illusion, predicated on repression of emotion. Remember to separate interpretation and opinion, both your own and that of others, from neutral consideration of data. Instead of real research, many people get stuck in the trap of looking only for information that confirms their prejudices.

Many people say they are thinking when they are only rearranging their prejudices.
—William James

LOVE THE GAME, LOVE THE PEANUT

Chess is a game of problem solving. Grand masters solve chess problems faster and in more ways than ordinary masters. In a classic study, Adrianus Dingeman deGroot, a Dutch researcher, found that the difference between chess masters and grand masters could not be traced to any disparity in intellectual endowment. The distinguishing characteristic of the grand masters was their love of the game. They played more, thought about it more frequently, and were more passionately involved in chess than the masters.

George Washington Carver, best known for the many uses of peanuts he discovered, was a master question asker and problem solver who strove to find ways to improve the quality of life for poor farmers. Carver attracted the attention of scientists who sought the secret of his remarkable inventiveness. Asked for the key to his scientific method, he replied, "First, you must love the peanut!"

This level of involvement and absorption is characteristic of geniuses in all walks of life. Whatever your problems or challenges, you dramatically increase your chances of solving them by committing yourself to do so. Commitment acts as a unifying force of mind, bringing out your best, helping you access deeper perceptions and latent abilities. Einstein attributed his success not to any special talent or mental power but to "curiosity, obsession, and dogged endurance." Thomas Edison proclaimed that genius was a function of "1 percent inspiration, 99 percent perspiration." When someone called his work the result of "Godlike genius," Edison responded, "Godlike genius, Godlike nothing . . . sticking to it is the genius."

Alexander Hamilton observed: "Men give me credit for some genius. All the genius I have lies in this; when I have a subject in hand, I study it profoundly. Day and night it is before me. My mind becomes pervaded with it. Then the effort that I have made is what people are pleased to call the fruit of genius. It is the fruit of labor and thought."

MIND MAP THE PROBLEM

A problem well formulated is almost solved. One of the best ways to formulate your problem is to mind map it. Begin by drawing a symbol in the center of a page that represents your problem or question. Then print the key words representing the classic elementary questions on lines radiating from the central image. Add a main branch for "Mental Set," "Emotions," and "Research." Then explore each branch. Mind mapping helps you appreciate the complexities of your problem; highlighting relationships between different elements and integrating the details in a big picture.

Sometimes, your initial problem-definition map will lead you directly to a solution. Dr. Madhu Jayawant, a senior chemist and research fellow for a leading chemical company, offers this example: "I used mind mapping to integrate a large amount of apparently unrelated data on a pulp-bleaching process. I put the data on a mind map, and as I began to make connections between the various elements of the process, I identified and defined an invention." The process took him less than one hour and was the key to the new invention.

Of course, solutions don't always come so easily. In many instances you will need to proceed to the generation phase.

Generation: Genuine Geniuses Generate

Generation comes from the same Latin root as genius—*gignere*—meaning to beget or produce. In the generation phase of the solution-finding process, we aim to beget or produce new perspectives. This phase is what people usually are referring to when they talk about brainstorming.

The Enchanted Loom: Your Creativity Data Base

After many attempts to discover a "memory center" in the brain, researchers have concluded that memory is not localized. Rather, it is spread throughout the brain in a staggeringly complex neural network. Nobel Prize–winning neurophysiologist Sir Charles Sherrington describes this as "an enchanted loom."

This network has a virtually limitless capacity to store and recall information.

All your memories are woven together through networks of association. Everything you remember is remembered in relationship to another memory. So the more you know, the more you can know. And, the more you know, the more you know there is to know. One secret of cultivating a good memory is learning to energize your knowledge through free-association.

In 1879, scientist Sir Francis Gaulton took a stroll down a London street. As he walked, he allowed his mind to associate freely with everything he saw. He counted about 300 objects and noted a multitude of associations with each one. One association led to another and another and another. "Samples of my whole life passed before me," he wrote. "Many bygone incidents, which I had never suspected to have formed part of my stock of thoughts, had been glanced at as objects too familiar to awaken the attention. I saw at once that the brain was vastly more active than I had previously believed it to be. And I was perfectly amazed at the unexpected width of the field of its everyday operations."

If you explore your associations as Gaulton did, you will remember things that would otherwise seem inaccessible. Several years ago, I was away for a weekend when I got a call from a friend who had just bought a new house and had three days to have a house inspection conducted. She was interested in hiring an inspection firm I had used when I had bought my home the previous year. When she first asked me on the phone, I had no idea of the housing inspector's name or his employer's. If I didn't know about the power of association, I probably would have said, "Sorry, I don't remember."

Instead, I asked her to give me a few minutes to do an associative search. I began by trying to remember anything at all concerning the inspection of my house. The first association that arose was a picture of myself standing on the front lawn, with the inspector looking up at the roof, telling me it might need to be replaced. This was an outstanding association, since a new roof would be expensive.

In my mind's eye, I continued on an associational tour of the house with the inspector. My train of association moved through the kitchen, down into the basement, and then to the water main. In the flow of the association, the house inspector put a sticker on the water main valve. As he did, I remembered a name written on it: Home Check Inspectors. I called my friend back and told her the name.

Your knowledge is much more than whatever you instantly recall. As you begin to understand this, you greatly mobilize your intelligence. When people say "I don't know" or "I don't remember," often what they really mean is that the information isn't immediately available. But if you stop and conduct a search, following the flow of your associations, you usually find that you do remember and you do know. The more you have this positive experience, the more your confidence will build. The more you build confidence in the power of associative thinking, the more you can access it for purposes of recall, creativity, and communication.

To conduct a fruitful associative search you must be willing to embrace the tension of not knowing. This becomes easier to do as you cultivate an awareness of your brain's amazing potential and design. The fear of getting the wrong answer forces many people to be intolerant of the uncertainty that accompanies real thinking. This intolerance preempts the creative associational guesswork that is a key element of higher intellectual functioning.

THE CHUTZPAH PRINCIPLE OF INTELLIGENCE

The willingness to venture a guess wakes up your brain's vast associational capacity. I call this the chutzpah principle of intelligence. *Chutzpah* is a Yiddish word that can be interpreted to mean courage or "nerve" in the face of uncertainty. Thinkers with chutzpah make a habit of conducting an associational search when presented with a question or challenge for which an answer is not immediately available. When your first reaction to a problem is "Gee, I don't know," you can awaken your natural associational power by asking, "Well, if I did know, what would I say?"

Nobel Prize–winning physicist Richard Feynman provides a wonderful example of the potency of chutzpah. As a member of the team of scientists working on the Manhattan project, he offered significant theoretical underpinnings for the design of the plant that produced fissionable material for the atomic bomb. When the engineers presented him with the plans for the plant Feynman was faced with a quandary— he didn't know the meaning of the symbols on the blueprints. Although the engineers had offered a brief explanation Feynman missed a few key elements (he was daydreaming!) and neglected to ask for an explanation. Embarrassed, he conducted a quick associational search and decided to guess the identity of one of the symbols on the plans. As he describes it, "I take my finger and I put it down on one of the mysterious little crosses in the middle of one of the blueprints, and I say, "What happens if this valve gets stuck? Figuring they're going to say, 'That's not a valve, sir, that's a window.' " It turns out that the mysterious cross *was* a valve and that Feynman's question was critical to the safe construction of the plant. The engineers were astonished by Feynman's ability to read their blueprint, calling his guess "fantastic" and a work of "genius."

Feynman's chutzpah was complemented with a great deal of study and knowledge. There is, of course, a critical difference between an informed guess, creative association, intelligent speculation, and total rubbish. Nevertheless, you can make dramatic improvements in your ability to solve problems by awakening your virtually unlimited capacity for association with a little chutzpah.

GET YOUR FEET WET

Generation is a function of letting your mind go. As your mind flows freely, you create new patterns of association that invite the "Aha!" of insight. Generation disrupts automatic mental sets to liberate new possibilities. That sounds easy, but habitual patterns are doggedly persistent. Most people respond to the request, "associate freely," with a blank stare. Our reluctance to associate freely can be traced to our fear of embarrassment and of being judged by others.

Most of us invest tremendous energy in ensuring that we are never perceived as foolish, silly, or just plain crazy. We internalize these fears so that even when alone we are unable to let our minds go free. In the generation phase, it is essential to allay the fear of judgment. To liberate new pathways required for insight, we must be willing to explore foolish, silly, and even seemingly crazy ideas.

Crazy people who are productive are geniuses. Crazy people who are rich are eccentric. Crazy people who are neither productive nor rich are just plain crazy. Geniuses and crazy people are both out in the middle of a deep ocean; geniuses swim, crazy people drown. Most of us are sitting safely on the shore. This section will show you how to get your feet wet.

Genius is the art of nonhabitual thought.
—*William James*

MOVE BEYOND BRAIN GROOVES

Each of us has a vast potential for creative thought. According to Dr. Deepak Chopra, human beings tend to think, on average, about 60,000 thoughts per day, but at least 95 percent of our thoughts are the same as they were the previous day.

We are all prone to get stuck in unproductive, automatic patterns of association—"brain grooves" that limit our perception, freedom, and creativity.

In a seminar in northern Virginia, police officers were discussing the nature of associative thinking, when one officer commented on his partner's habit of association. Every day they would drive past a particular corner where his partner had some childhood experiences. And every day, when they reached that spot, the partner would begin to talk about the same thing. All of a sudden, the officer who was complaining about his partner realized that, every day, *he* had the same reaction to his partner's habitual association. This minienlightenment gave him insight into his potential for the freedom to choose his response to what had previously been an unconscious habitual pattern.

You can free yourself from brain grooves by stimulating your mind with novelty. Read novels. Visit new places, especially foreign countries. Try new foods. Drive to work a different way. One of the richest sources of fresh associations comes from meeting different types of people. As we get older, most of us interact primarily with people from similar socioeconomic and professional backgrounds. To prevent this intellectual inbreeding from retarding your freedom of association, make an effort to meet people from other groups, backgrounds, and perspectives. It is especially valuable to spend time with children.

Author Ray Bradbury offers a delightful perspective on nurturing freshness of mind: "You have to feed yourself . . . every day, with all kinds of material from various fields, outrageous fields. I stuff my eyeballs with paintings and lithographs, listen to music, read essays, poetry, plays. . . . When I was a kid, I sneaked over to the grown-up section in the library. Now, I go into the children's section, to make sure that I'm fully informed."

More important than the external stimulus that may bring you a new track of associations is your willingness to embrace the unknown. Look for different things but remember to look at things differently. In the words of Marcel Proust: "The real magic lies not in seeing new landscapes, but in having new eyes." See the world afresh every day. Think, Today I will think new thoughts, create new associations, develop new, broader perspectives. I will approach the world in a deeper, truer, richer way. You will begin to expand your perception.

The uniqueness and unlimited potential for association of each person means that any group of people can provide a powerful resource for problem solving and brainstorming. A weakness in most brainstorming approaches is that groups get together with the idea of letting their ideas flow freely, but everyone follows the associations of the most extroverted, expressive or authoritative person in the group.

The most effective way to organize a brainstorm, problem solving, or planning session is to begin by having each individual independently generate his or her own thoughts. Then move into small groups and nurture the ideas further before presenting them to the larger group. This is the **greenhouse theory of creativity.** Ideas start as delicate, little seedlings that need to be carefully nurtured on an individual basis. Then they can be put into bigger pots in the greenhouse—the equivalent of small groups—and then they're ready to live in the real garden.

GO FOR QUANTITY!

If you've targeted a well-framed question and are approaching it with an open, questing mind-set, then you've established fertile ground for new ideas. If you throw one seed on that ground your chances for new growth are slim. If you throw a hundred your chances improve. Throw a thousand and you'll probably be able to look forward to a rich harvest.

The more ideas you generate, the greater your chances for a breakthrough. Thousands of silly, useless, and wrong ideas fertilize the blossoming of one really good idea. Generating lots of ideas pushes you outside habitual patterns and exponentially increases the possibility of making new connections.

> *If you want to get a good idea, get a lot of ideas.*
> *—Dr. Linus Pauling, two-time Nobel Prize winner*

ENCOURAGE HUMOR

In the generation phase, the more ideas the merrier. And the merrier the ideas the better. A number of experiments have shown that humor improves scores on creativity tests. In the classic version, three groups receive a battery of creativity tests. Before the tests, the first group listens to comedy tapes. The second group listens to tapes on an academic subject. The third group just sits around. Invariably, the comedy group scores highest.

Trish Marosky, a district manager for a major pharmaceutical company, takes her staff to Chicago's famous Second City improvisational comedy shows and arranges for them to have lessons in improvisation. "We are invariably more productive, more creative, as a result of immersing ourselves in spontaneous humor," she says.

Humor echoes and supports the process of creative thinking. It reduces stress and promotes relaxed concentration and higher brain thinking. Moreover, the essence of humor is a shift of expectation, a juxtaposition of previously unrelated elements. For example, comic genius Stephen Wright deadpans, "I was walking down the street one day and I passed a restaurant. The sign in the window said 'Breakfast Anytime.' So I went in and ordered ham and eggs in the Renaissance."

By playing with our expectations and shifting us out of habitual thought patterns, Wright and other humorists evoke laughter. "Ha ha" is the first cousin of aha! The most creative and successful people are those who laugh regularly—particularly those who can laugh at themselves.

SUSPEND THE EXPRESSION OF JUDGMENT

In *Good Morning, Vietnam,* Robin Williams played the role of a wartime disk jockey with a tendency to share his hilariously cynical views with listeners. Williams's material had to be approved by robot-like, identical twin censors who were driven to apoplexy in their attempt to police him.

The theme of art versus censorship is a common one in cinema, literature, and life. It reflects the conflict between artist and censor that we carry inside our minds. For most of us, the artist is repressed and the censor is hyperactive. Although the censor is a valuable ally in daily life (can you imagine how disastrous it would be if we always said exactly what we're thinking?), in the generation phase, the censor is off duty. It's time for the artist to play.

Many people pay lip service to the idea of "no evaluation," and then proceed to mock others as soon as anything really different is expressed. Comments like, "That's stupid," "When we asked for creative ideas, we didn't mean *that* creative," "What kind of weirdo are you anyway?" and "Let's not waste our time on absurd speculation," have no place in the generation mode. Insidiously, many people express their hyperactive censor by aiming sidelong, withering glances and dismissive gestures at purveyors of "off-the-wall" ideas.

One technique for stopping inappropriate censoring is to crumple up sheets of paper and toss them at violators of the process. Advertising mastermind Alex Osborn, creator of the concept of brainstorming, liked to ring a bell to ward off overanxious critics. Perhaps the most effective way is to remind them that the role of critic is valuable but that *this is not the time for it.* Emphasize that the task at hand is to act out a role that calls for the suspension of ordinary logic.

Asking people to act out a role is one of the most effective ways to get their creative juices flowing. Many critical, serious people find that the opportunity to play a role frees them from their habitual mode of thinking. Critics are usually highly competitive and if you inspire them to compete at coming up with lots of off-the-wall ideas they will amaze you, and themselves.

DESCARTES MEETS CHUBBY CHECKER

Quantity, humor, and suspension of judgment energize the creative process. But we often need more aggressive approaches to get our minds moving. Descartes proclaimed *"Cogito ergo sum"*—"I think therefore I am." *Cogito* comes from the Latin *coagitare,* "to shake together." Chubby Checker offered a new twist on Cartesian philosophy, "Shake it up, baby . . . work it on out!" (Chubby's identity emerged from a creative restructuring of his idol, Fats Domino.)

In the creative process we work things out by shaking them up. Creative thinking involves linking ideas, facts, perception, and associative patterns in unfamiliar ways. How can you shake up your mind to combine and relate ideas in new ways? Try these methods:

Make a mind map
Read and make up Koans
Ask, "what if?"
Bring in an outsider
Put on a new head
Become the question
Pull the cow by the tail
Write down the bones
Experiment with visual synthesis and image-streaming
Awaken synaesthesia
Change your position

Make a Mind Map. Mind mapping is an effective idea-generating tool. By starting with a picture or symbol, you jump-start the right hemisphere while the branching format encourages free-association. Traditional brainstorming sessions usually result in tons of disconnected ideas written on flip charts. By printing key words, one per line, and keeping the lines connected, mind mapping helps you track and enhance the flow of ideas. If you run out of ideas for your mind map, pause, take a deep breath, and then print random words to open up new pathways. You can also take any key word on your map and draw three blank lines radiating from it. The mind's natural tendency to complete a gestalt will inspire you to fill the lines with new associations.

Generating ideas with mind mapping is a lot like distance running. If you are an inexperienced runner, chances are that you will give up when you feel winded. Experienced runners know, however, that if they remain relaxed and keep their arms and legs moving, they will find their second wind, running farther and faster than they may have felt possible. It's the same with creative thinking. If you feel "mentally winded," stay relaxed and keep your mind moving by printing key words and drawing symbols, even if they seem totally irrelevant. You will discover your mental second wind generating whole new streams of association.

Moreover, the later stages of the generation phase are usually the most productive. Brainstormers often find that they must first burst out all their standard thoughts and habitual responses before discovering new pathways.

Read and Make Up Koans. Koans are teaching tools used in Zen and other Eastern philosophies. Examples include the classics, "What is the sound of one hand clapping?" and "Why does the perfect circle have no circumference?" These one-line riddles are used to challenge habitual thinking and spur the adept to enlightenment. A client in the fashion retail business generated "merchandising enlightenment" by asking his sales team, "What does clothing wear?"

Q: How many Zen masters does it take to change a light bulb?
A: Two—one to do it and one to not do it.

You can lead a horse to water but a pencil has to be lead.

Ask, What If? "What if" questions stimulate your imagination and shake up your perspective. Ask what if I: shrunk it, enlarged it, made it lighter, heavier, changed its shape, reversed it, tightened it, loosened it, added something, subtracted something, interchanged parts, stayed open twenty-four hours, guaranteed it, changed its name, made it recyclable, stronger, weaker, softer, harder, portable, immovable, doubled the price, or paid customers to take it?

The multibillion-dollar economy of Silicon Valley was largely inspired by the question, "*What if* we shrunk it (computer chips)?" The craze for offering rebates as a sales incentive was born from the question, "*What if* we paid our customers to buy it?" The happiest people in the world ask, "*What if* I could find some way to get paid for doing what I love?"

Bring in an Outsider. Consult someone with an entirely different perspective. Ask the opinion of people from other departments, backgrounds, disciplines, and thinking styles. Ask your bus driver and your dentist. Ask the oldest person you know, and the youngest.

Children can offer amazing insights. As physicist Robert Oppenheimer commented, "There are children playing in the street who could solve some of my top problems in physics because they have modes of perception that I lost long ago."

Put on a New Head. Other people aren't always available when you need them. Nevertheless, you can try to imagine what they'd say if they were present. By using your imagination, you can create a superpowered internal advisory board. Ask, "What would Walt Disney (43), Lillian Hellman, Muhammad Ali (32), Margaret Thatcher, Gary Kasparov, Jean-Luc Picard, Robin Williams, Ben Franklin (29), Helen Keller, Buddha, William Shakespeare (2), Barbara Walters, Mark Twain, Morihei Ueshiba (44), Winston Churchill, and Marcel Marceau say about this?"

Creativity guru Dr. Win Wenger suggests that we go further than just imagining what our "advisers" might say. He advocates visualizing an image of the genius we wish to consult. Then walk into the space occupied by this image and imagine putting on the genius's head. Try it, it works.

Become the Question. When Jonas Salk was working on a polio vaccine, he imagined himself as an immune system, and contemplated how to fight the virus from that perspective. Einstein's insights that led to his theory of relativity resulted from his "becoming" light.

A restaurant client was inspired to design a successful new menu by contemplating the question, "Imagine you are an item on a menu—how could you get people to order you?" To solve the problem of how to play better tennis, Tim Gallwey, the author of *The Inner Game of Tennis,* urges "become the tennis ball—put your consciousness in the ball and ride across the net."

Pull the Cow by the Tail. Dr. Milton Erickson developed a fascinating and effective psychotherapeutic approach based on stimulating new patterns of thought and behavior through the consideration of paradox. Erickson claimed that his approach was born when he was an eight-year-old farmboy trying to help his brothers pull a cow into a stall. After the brothers gave up yanking on the stubborn cow's head, little Milton pulled its tail and the cow went straight into the stall.

Try pulling the tail of your problem. Take a break from looking for solutions and look for ways to make the problem worse. If you are trying to improve communication at work, for example, experiment with thinking of everything you could do to undermine it: spread rumors and gossip, insist on lengthy written reports, discourage informal, social interaction, practice bad listening, avoid performance reviews, don't give feedback, and never ask for help.

An Environmental Protection Agency office in New England demonstrated a delightful expression of tail-pulling through a public awareness program titled, "How to Destroy the Earth." They offered tongue-in-cheek suggestions such as: dump used motor oil straight into the ground, leave your lights and air conditioner on at all times, stuff your newspapers, cans, and bottles into the same garbage bag. . . .

Write Down the Bones. Natalie Goldberg, the author of *Writing Down the Bones*, has spent decades applying the wisdom of Zen Buddhism to learning and teaching writing. In the process, she developed a method that awakens deep levels of creative thinking. After reading a few chapters of Goldberg's book, her friend John Rollwagen, the president of Cray Research, commented: "Why, Natalie, you're talking about business." Goldberg's method is simple:

- Dedicate a set time for writing. Ten-minute sessions are good to start.
- Write continuously. Keep your pen moving.
- Don't edit.
- Ignore punctuation, grammar, spelling, and neatness.
- Avoid doing what you normally call thinking.
- Let yourself go.
- Describe things in rich detail.
- Follow your passions.

Goldberg suggests a variety of stimulating writing topics, ranging from books that have changed your life and the quality of light coming through your window, to the closest you ever felt to God or nature and your first sexual experience.

After warming up with a couple of exercises on whatever topics you fancy, try "writing down the bones" of the problem or question you aim to resolve. Goldberg urges, "Explore the rugged edge of thought. Like grating a carrot, give the paper the colorful coleslaw of your consciousness." Conscientiously applying her method, you will peel away layers of censorial thinking and discover your raw originality.

VISUAL SYNTHESIS AND IMAGE STREAMING

The word *imagination* comes from the root *imaginari*, which means "to picture internally." Our ability to form and express internal pictures holds a special key to creative thinking. Creativity often springs from a realm that is beyond words. By accessing preverbal levels of mind, we awaken spontaneous insight.

In a landmark survey of the working methods of great mathematicians, Dr. Jacques Hadmard found that their thinking process was characterized not by language or standard mathematical symbols but rather by visual imagery. Einstein, one of the mathematicians who participated, wrote: "The words of the language as they are written or spoken do not seem to play any role in my mechanism of thought, which relies on more or less clear images of a visual and some of a muscular type."

An advanced and highly effective form of creative mind mapping, involves accessing and expressing our preverbal intelligence by representing ideas *primarily* in pictures and symbols. Try exploring your problems and questions by free-associating through drawing.

Image maps are particularly powerful tools. In 1992, a group of nine of the country's leading pharmacists and three pharmaceutical company product managers took part in a brainstorming session at the company headquarters. The aim was to generate new ideas on how to collaborate to better serve patients.

After a minicourse in solution finding, the session began by applying the "greenhouse" approach to idea generation. The participants were asked to generate ideas individually before sharing them in small groups. As each group spokesperson presented the fruits of their process, artist Nusa Maal Gelb represented their words in evocative imagery on giant sheets of paper taped to the walls. Nusa calls this process visual synthesis. As the participants saw their concepts translated into pictures, they were inspired to develop new insights and connections. Try drawing the images that you associate with a problem you wish to solve. Nancy Margulies, author of *Mapping Inner Space,* offers a delightful name for this process of pictorial mind mapping, she calls it: "Mindscaping."

If you are not comfortable drawing images, you can still benefit from their power simply by describing them aloud to a friend or into a tape recorder, as they occur to you. To do this, relax, enjoy deep rhythmic breathing, and close your eyes. As images, however vague, arise in your mind's eye, begin describing them in detail. Dr. Win Wenger, creator of this "image streaming" method, has documented its effectiveness in generating insight.

AWAKEN SYNAESTHESIA

Synaesthesia, the merging of the senses, is a trade secret of highly creative people. The greatest artists and scientists cultivated their synaesthetic capacities. You can, too.

Think of your problem. Give it a color and shape. Imagine what it smells and tastes like. How does it feel? What are the textures and sounds of your possible solutions? Does this seem crazy?

Consider Nobel Prize winner Richard Feynman's description of his method for analyzing complex theorems: "As they are telling me the conditions of the theorem, I construct something which fits all the conditions. You know, you have a set (one ball)—disjoint (two balls). Then the balls turn colors, grow hairs, or whatever in my head as they put more conditions on. Finally they state the theorem, which is some dumb thing about the ball which isn't true for my hairy green ball thing, so I say, 'False!' I guessed right most of the time."

Benoit Mandelbrot, creator of fractal geometry adds, "Geometry is sensual, one touches things. . . . I see things before I formulate them. . . . Intuition is not something that is given. I've trained my intuition to accept as obvious shapes which were initially rejected as absurd, and I find everyone else can do the same. These shapes provide a handle to representing nature. . . ."

Cultivating synaesthesia not only enhances creativity but also deepens and enriches the quality of life. My wife is an artist and naturally synaesthetic. One late autumn morning we were watching the leaves outside our window gently rustle in the breeze. My wife exclaimed, "The leaves are tickling me." At that moment I experienced the leaves in a whole new way. Their color and texture became vibrantly alive as I allowed myself to "feel" their motion.

Painter Lorraine Gill is renowned for her penetrating abstractions that probe the collective unconscious. One afternoon at her home, when I was her guest at lunch, she prepared a simple vegetable stew. Just before we began eating, she asked, "Would you mind if I sing the colors of our lunch?" She pointed to the carrots and sang the tone she heard when she saw them. She did the same for the red peppers and the eggplant. Through her eyes and voice, vegetables were transformed into melodic gems.

CHANGE YOUR POSITION

In many brainstorming sessions people sit around for hours, in more or less the same position, trying to generate ideas. And then they ask, "Why are we stuck?"

The state of your body influences your mind. If your body is stiff and rigid, or collapsed and limp, your mind will often follow suit. Our language is full of phrases that demonstrate an understanding of this relationship: "She won't change her *position* on this issue," "They've taken an aggressive *stance* on this point," "Perhaps we should look at this from another *angle*." And from the Bible, "They stiffened their necks so they would not hear the word of the Lord."

Letting go of habitual postures energizes and inspires the creative process. Sometimes the best way to get your mind moving is to start by moving your body. My favorite methods include juggling, movements from the martial art of aikido, application of the Alexander technique (see the Bibliography for references on how you can learn these three disciplines) and the following exercise that you can try with a friend (if you are alone, then do it in front of a mirror): the object is to move as many body parts as possible, in new ways, at the same time.

The exercise leads you to change habitual body-mind positions, by moving in a way that you have never moved before.

Stand opposite your partner. You are going to copy the movements that your partner makes. Your partner begins, for example, by raising her right hand and patting her head, then dropping her hand back to her side. Copy the movement and keep doing it while you wait for your partner to introduce the next movement. For the next movement your partner taps her left foot. Copy this movement while continuing with the previous one. Next, your partner makes a swimming motion with her left arm. Copy this while continuing the two previous movements. Then, your partner adds a sound like a chicken noise or the theme from *The Twilight Zone*. Copy the sound and continue the previous movements. Then, she rotates her head around in a big circle, and so on.

Aim to do at least five different movements at once. Make them as unusual and absurd as possible. Then switch roles and lead your partner to make movements even sillier than the ones you just finished making. In addition to raising the level of laughter and fun dramatically, this exercise shakes up old patterns and wakes up new connections.

THE HEART OF SYNVERGENT THINKING

Sometimes the generation phase of the solution-finding process results in an immediate breakthrough—the "Aha" of insight and illumination. Frequently, however, it leads to an increased sense of chaos, confusion, and frustration. One of the most important things to understand about the problem-solving/solution-finding process is that the experience of increased uncertainty is a positive sign.

If you have successfully shifted out of habitual perceptual and intellectual patterns, you may feel somewhat anxious. *The willingness to accept and embrace this inner tension is the most distinguishing characteristic of highly creative people.* It is the heart of synvergent thinking. It is much easier to face uncertainty with confidence if you understand that your mind is designed to translate your heightened state of "cogitation" into insights and solutions. This translation takes place in the incubation phase of the process.

Incubation : Sleep on It

Have you ever solved a problem by sleeping on it? What's going on in your mind when you are not consciously working on a problem? In the incubation phase, your subattentional mind sorts through all the data you've collected, all the possibilities you've played with, and puts it all together.

Great musicians claim that their art comes to life in the spaces between notes. Master sculptors point to the space around their work as the secret of its power. Similarly, the spaces between your conscious efforts provide a key to the art of creative problem solving. These spaces allow ideas to incubate.

Mathematician Henri Poincaré called incubation "unconscious work," and described it this way: "Often when one works hard at a question, nothing good is accomplished at the first attack. Then one takes a rest . . . and sits down anew to the work . . . and then all of a sudden the decisive idea presents itself to the mind. . . . These sudden inspirations never happen except after some days of voluntary effort which has appeared absolutely fruitless. . . . These efforts have not been as sterile as one thinks; they have set agoing the unconscious mind."

The incubation mode is most effective when we alternate, as Poincaré suggests, between periods of intense focus and rest. Without periods of intense focus, there is nothing to be incubated, nothing to set the unconscious mind "agoing."

Discovering and learning to trust your incubatory rhythms makes creative problem solving more efficient and enjoyable. As the philosopher Bertrand Russell observed: "I have found . . . that if I have to write upon some difficult topic, the best plan is to think about it with very great intensity—the greatest intensity of which I am capable—for a few hours or days, and at the end of that time, give orders, so to speak, that the work is to proceed underground. After some months, I return consciously to the topic and find that the work has been done. Before I had discovered this technique, I used to spend the intervening months worrying because I was making no progress. I arrived at the solution none the sooner for this worry, and the intervening months were wasted, whereas now I can devote them to other pursuits."

Sometimes incubation yields an obvious insight, or Aha! But frequently the fruits of our unconscious work are subtle and easy to overlook. Excellence in creative problem solving requires that we cultivate attention to the delicate nuances of thought, listening for the faint whispers of shy inner voices. Hotelier Conrad Hilton comments, "I know when I have a problem and have done all I can to figure it out, I keep listening in a sort of inside silence, till something clicks and I feel a right answer."

One of the joys of collecting wine is knowing that as time passes fine wines get better. Thanks to the power of incubation, the same is true about ideas.

Brain researchers estimate that your unconscious data base outweighs the conscious on an order exceeding ten million to one. This data base is the source of your hidden, natural genius. In other words, a part of you is much smarter than you are. The wisest people regularly consult that smarter part!

The human mind is designed by millions of years of evolution to be the most profoundly powerful creative problem-solving system in creation. As we gain confidence in our brain's natural solution-finding power, we are better able to heed the advice of Emerson, offered in his magnificent essay, "Self Reliance": "We should learn to detect and watch that gleam of light which flashes across our own minds." Emerson warns against the tendency to sell ourselves short: "[If] we dismiss without notice our own thoughts; they come back to us with a certain alienated majesty. Tomorrow a stranger will say with good sense precisely what we have thought and felt all the time, and we shall be forced to take with shame our own opinion from another."

No idea is so outlandish that it should not be considered with a searching but at the same time steady eye.
—Winston Churchill

Balancing generation and incubation will move you beyond habitual ways of thinking, beckoning you to enter a world of unlimited possibilities. In the real world, however, some possibilities are clearly better than others. In the evaluation phase, we expose our ideas to "a searching but . . . steady eye."

Evaluation: Hooking the Fish

Buckminster Fuller said, "I call intuition cosmic fishing. You feel a nibble, then you've got to hook the fish." After baiting the hook through preparation and generation and trolling deep waters with incubation, it is time to reel in the catch.

The first step in the evaluation phase is to organize and prioritize the ideas you have generated by making a mind map of all your proposed solutions—this lets you process a tremendous amount of information at a glance. It helps you see relationships and discover connections, making it easier to consolidate the best elements of a number of different solutions. Using color or symbol codes also makes it easier to prioritize your ideas.

Once you've put your ideas in order, subject them to cross-examination by playing the following roles:

Angel's Advocate. When I started my career, I was inspired by what now seems like incredibly naive, do-gooder optimism. I had this crazy idea that if I followed what I was most interested in—things that benefit my own personal growth and the growth of others—that everything would work out fine. Amazingly, that's just what happened.

Cynics define an optimist as someone lacking all the facts. Like many people who succeed, I didn't know that my chances were slim. Perhaps if I had "all the facts," I would have chosen a more secure path.

Speculative, optimistic thinking is the source of all accomplishment and an integral part of creative problem solving. In the angel's advocate role, focus on the bright side of the idea in question. Translate your idea into positive proposals and constructive suggestions. Engage in positive speculation, focusing on benefits and opportunities. Paint utopian scenarios and show how they can be realized. Express everything positive about the idea, all its strengths and the reasons it will work.

True positive thinking is a discipline. It is much easier to cut an idea down than to build one up, which is why it's best to play angel first. Of course, it is also essential to learn how to whittle ideas into shape.

Devil's Advocate. In my work with management teams, I often find that in the course of decision-making sessions, someone says, "Let me play the role of devil's advocate." Afterward, this person makes an all-out effort to trash whatever creative ideas have been offered. More devil than advocate, these individuals take a special joy in throwing out the baby with the bathwater.

If an idea is 80 percent right and 20 percent wrong it is essential to target the 20 percent and find a way to fix it. As Edward de Bono notes, what frequently happens instead is a hyperactive pouncing on the weakness of the 20 percent accompanied by an implication that whoever proposed that 20 percent must be a complete fool. And that, since the remaining 80 percent was put forward by a fool, it must also be wrong.

The devil's advocate role is an essential element in creative problem solving, but it is easily warped by the reptilian drive for one-upmanship. Putting an idea down offers the promise of higher status in the hierarchy, whereas supporting something new is a much riskier, more vulnerable position.

The art of useful negative thinking requires separating emotions, egotism and personal, inflammatory language from logical, critical assessment. An effective devil's advocate acknowledges and suspends emotional reactions to an idea before pointing out: reasons it will not work; weaknesses, gaps, and inadequacies; hazards, risks, and liabilities; everything that can possibly go wrong; consequences of failure; costs and difficulties of implementation; questionable data and unproven assumptions; potentially adverse legal and ethical implications; and faulty logic.

Thorough cross-examination by the devil's advocate may expose the weaknesses of an idea and inspire you to modify and strengthen it accordingly. It may send you back to the drawing board, specifically back to the preparation or generation modes. Or it may confirm that you are on the right track and build confidence in your idea. You can be certain, however, that if you don't play this role, then reality will ultimately do it for you.

The Judge. After your advocates have made their case, send it to your inner judge for deliberation. Make a comprehensive mind map for each idea, including branches such as:

Outcome:	What is the idea supposed to achieve or accomplish?
Set:	What assumptions, prejudices, paradigms, or mental sets influence you?
Strengths:	Advantages of the proposed solution, benefits, summary of angel's case.
Weaknesses:	Disadvantages of the idea, costs, summary of devil's case.
Interesting:	Aspects of the idea and its possible consequences that are neither positive or negative just interesting.
Timing:	Is there a deadline? Is this the time for your idea? What will happen if you do nothing?
Market:	Who is the audience, client, or customer for your idea?
Success:	What are your criteria for success and failure? How will you know that you have succeeded?

After you consider every aspect of the proposed solution, it is time to decide. Ultimately, our decisions are influenced by our values, and our values are deeply laden with emotion. Having held your feelings in abeyance to objectively map your thoughts, this is the time to put them on the table. The bottom line of effective decision making is: *integrate all relevant information and then "trust your gut."*

Make a mind map of your ideas and submit it to your judge.

In the study of ideas, it is necessary to remember that insistence on hard-headed clarity issues from sentimental feeling. Insistence on clarity at all costs is based on sheer superstition as to the mode in which human intelligence functions. Our reasonings grasp at straws for premises and float on gossamers for deductions.
—A. N. Whitehead

In the words of management genius Alfred Sloane, "The final act of business judgment is intuitive." Prof. Weston Agor, author of *The Logic of Intuitive Decision-Making,* discovered through extensive interviews that senior executives overwhelmingly pointed to a failure to heed their own intuition as the prime cause of their worst decisions.

In 1960, Ray Kroc's lawyers advised him against spending nearly $3 million on a couple of burger joints and the rights to the McDonald's name. Kroc stated that his "funny bone" told him to overrule his counsel and make the deal.

How can you learn to trust your funny bone? The same way that you get to Carnegie Hall—practice. Bring more attention to your everyday hunches and intuitions. Try writing them down and then checking your accuracy. What will the weather be like tomorrow? What would someone close to you really love for a birthday present? What kind of mood will your boss be in today? Which way will interest rates move in the next three months? By monitoring your daily intuitions, you hone their accuracy. Check historically when you have felt an intuition—were you accurate?

Cultivating a reliable inner guidance system requires listening to your body. Comments such as, "My gut tells me otherwise," "I just know it in my bones," "I can feel it in the pit of my stomach," or "I know in my heart of hearts that it must be true" reflect the body-centered nature of intuition.

Dr. Eugene Gendlin, the author of *Focusing*, offers a body-centered tool for checking intuitions. He calls it "instant hindsight." Gendlin advises: "You should say to yourself, as if it were true—this decision feels fine. The problem is solved and I feel good about it, don't I?" Gendlin counsels attending to whatever bodily sensations arise as these words are spoken; if the sensations are queasy or unpleasant, chances are you are off the mark; if the feelings engendered are pleasant, you are probably on course.

Intuition is not mystical extrasensory perception. It is logic working at a very high speed on a subattentional level. When an intuition proves to be accurate you can always track back and see why it made sense. Intuition is superlogic. It is only logical to learn to use it.

Implementation: Make It So

In *Star Trek: The Next Generation*, Capt. Jean-Luc Picard provides a marvelous example of creative leadership. Under conditions of extreme stress, a breakdown of the *Enterprise*'s core reactor or an impending assault by hostile aliens, Picard brings his staff together and encourages them to generate ideas. He integrates the analysis he receives from Commander Data with the intuitions of Lieutenant Troi. Then, after a decision is reached, he issues his famous command: "Make it so."

One weakness of many brainstorming efforts is that they end before anything is actually accomplished. People get together, dump lots of ideas on flip charts, hang them on the wall, and go home. They may have generated many potentially valuable ideas and had some good laughs, but without a focus on "making it so," nothing is created.

Making things happen effectively is a function of four simple ingredients.

1. **A vivid, positive vision of what you want.** Visualize your success as a "done deal." Create synaesthetic, multidimensional images of your vision already realized. See it, feel it, smell it, touch it, taste it, be it.

2. **An accurate perception of what you have.** Question your assumptions and mental sets. Seek objective feedback. Assess the resistance, competition, and other obstacles you must overcome or transform.

3. **A plan.** Plan backward—start with the realization of your goal and work your way to the present; then, set time lines. Think strategically and tactically. Line up allies, resources, sponsors, and supporters. Make a thoughtful plan and *be prepared to improvise.*

4. **Commitment and accountability.** Throw the full force of your being into achieving your aims. Act as though you are 100 percent responsible for the results.

Successful people know that it is easier to ask forgiveness than for permission. Many good ideas rot on the vine called "waiting for permission and approval." Other common strategies for *non*achievement include:

- Subject your idea to exhaustive analysis
- Wait for certainty
- Ignore other's interests

- Waffle on your commitment
- Make excuses
- Claim all the credit
- Assume that nothing will change
- Don't anticipate obstacles and resistance

The more innovative your action, the more resistance you can expect, especially in an organizational context. A new idea, no matter how positive its implications, always suggests abandonment of the old.

In the classic television show *All in the Family,* reactionary Archie Bunker responded to creative suggestions by his wife or son-in-law with, "Stifle yourself." Organizations are rife with Bunker-style reactions to innovation.

Resistance to creativity often takes the form of "Bunkerisms"— phrases designed to stifle new ideas. The top ten Bunkerisms I've heard over the years are:

10. "We've always done it this way."
9. "That's not how we do things around here."
8. "It's not in the budget."
7. "You have to prove that it will work before we try anything."
6. "If it ain't broke don't fix it."
5. "Yes, but . . ."
4. "We're not ready for that kind of change."
3. "Don't rock the boat."
2. "The lawyers won't like it."
1. "If that were such a good idea, someone would have already done it."

No matter how brilliant your idea, it remains dormant if you are unwilling to buck the tide of Bunkerism. Creativity requires the courage to move forward in the face of resistance. It demands that we access the role of "champion"—defined by Webster as "one who comes forward in defense of a person or cause, a vindicator or protector." Champions know that success is inevitable; that there is no such thing as failure, only feedback.

Before the struggle, victory is mine.
—Mitsugi Saotome, aikido master

A champion views resistance as a gift, helping to refine and strengthen the idea. Champions accept and transform the energy of resistance by looking beneath the knee-jerk expression of Bunkerisms to the real fears and concerns of all stakeholders. Armed with vision, empathy, and the skills of synvergent thinking, champions build support and make things happen.

Vindicator. Protector. Champion. Whatever we call it, we are really talking about leadership.

The Ultimate Secret of Success

To apply the phases of the solution-finding process, begin by focusing on preparation. Specifically, define your questions, conduct research, and commit to the process of finding a solution. From there, proceed to the generation mode. Move beyond your brain grooves by shaking up your mind. For maximum productivity in the generation mode, take brain breaks, thereby integrating incubation and generation.

If your generation/incubation process yields a new synthesis, "Aha!" insight or illumination, you'll probably want to proceed to the evaluation mode, where you begin analyzing and reality-testing your idea. If the generation mode results in a sense of greater chaos, confusion, or frustration, move back to the preparation mode and check your question or, move fully into incubation mode, allowing your subattentional intelligence to put it all together.

There are no set rules for the amount of time you spend in each phase. The time you devote will be a function of the total time available for solution finding. One error some people make in problem solving is to get together for just a morning or afternoon in an attempt to solve a significant problem. This does not leave enough time for incubation. Aim to conduct problem-solving/brainstorming sessions over the course of at least two days. The creativity and productivity of these sessions goes up dramatically when you allow time to literally sleep on the problem.

THE ULTIMATE CREATIVITY METHOD

When it comes to solving life's problems, from deciding to marry or choosing a career to designing a new product or creating a new organizational culture, one problem-solving approach reigns supreme: *ask for guidance* from a higher power. Whether you think of the higher power as divinely inspired or as an expression of your vast subattentional intelligence, *sincerely* asking for guidance liberates you from the constricting effects of the repto-mammalian mind. Prayer and deep contemplation open a channel to the source of creativity.

More than guidelines for running a problem-solving session, these phases represent the ingredients of a creative approach to life. Use this information to discover your own style and rhythm of creating.

As you develop and refine the life map discussed earlier, you will clarify the major questions that organize your sense of purpose. Your perceptions will follow your purposes. All of your life experiences can then serve as research toward the achievement of your goals. Every night's sleep and dreams can incubate your life questions.

Make a habit of generating nonhabitual ideas. Use the angel, devil, and judge in your everyday decision making. Be a champion for your family, organization, community, country, planet, and for yourself.

Creativity is not just the province of great artists, musicians, scientists, and business leaders. It is your birthright . . . the essence of living. Giving birth, forming a sentence, preparing a meal, growing a garden; our very existence is an expression of the creative force of the universe. Be a student of the creative force. Learn its laws. Harmonizing with the universe is the ultimate secret of success.

Those who are enlightened never stop forging themselves . . . the most perfect actions echo the patterns found in nature.
—Morihei Ueshiba, founder of aikido

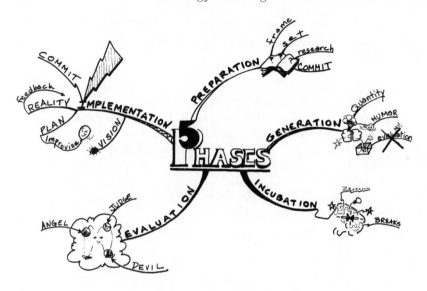

A mind map overview of the five phases of synvergent problem solving.

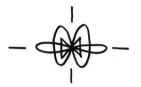

Part II

SYNVERGENT

COMMUNICATION

AND PRESENTATION

FOR LEADERSHIP

Chapter 4

— ✦ —

Synvergent Communication

"Old paradigm" hierarchical organizations feature "hording" of information by a handful of executives; specialized, independent functional units (departments) and one-way, formal, top-down communication. The evolving, streamlined, flexible model calls for broad sharing of information, interdependent high performance teams, and open, informal, multidirectional communication. A lot easier said than done.

If you think and communicate as you always have, you will get what
you have always gotten, regardless of the jargon you use.
—M. J. G.

Habits of hierarchical communication go hand-in-hand with habits of hierarchical thinking. In the first three chapters of *Thinking for a Change*, you learned how to apply synvergent thinking to awaken new skills of life balance, planning, and problem solving. In this section you will learn how to transform your approach to everyday communication and presentation by applying a synvergent perspective.

In my work with organizations, clients invariably rank communication problems at the top of their lists. And, most people acknowledge that they would be better off if they could improve communication with their spouses or children. In this chapter we will zero in on the essence of these issues, revealing a practical approach to bringing out the best in yourself and others. Let's begin with a simple exercise that illuminates the way the mind links ideas together.

Thinking Is Linking: Two Great Truths About People

Please complete this simple word association exercise: below is a circle with ten lines radiating from it. Copy this illustration on a blank sheet of paper.

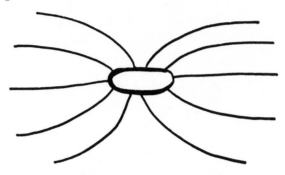

After you read the instructions, you will be given a word to write in the center of that circle. As soon as you've written that central word, write a word on each of the spokes that you associate with the word in the center. Put down your first ten associations with the word in the center as quickly as you can, without judging or editing. In a word association exercise there are no wrong answers.

Ready?

The word is: *dance.*

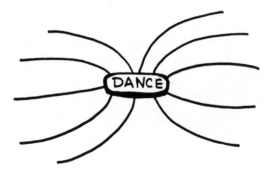

After you complete your ten word associations, consider what the associations of a friend or co-worker might be with the same word. How many words would you have in common with one of your peers, or your spouse, your best friend, or your boss? Most people are surprised to discover the differences that appear when they compare their results with others. It's rare for a group to have much in common at all.

In one group, for example, Jill's first word was *Baryshnikov*, the name of her favorite dancer. Joe's first association was *defense*, because he thought of the sack dance performed by successful linebackers. Betsy, whose daughter was about to graduate from high school wrote *prom* on her first spoke, while Jim, a budding poet, wrote *trance*. Their other nine words were equally diverse.

Typical results of the dance exercise.

Of course, occasionally people do get one or two words in common but when you explore the results further, and ask them to associate ten words with the shared word, you find that they usually meant something different by the common word after all.

When a group of accountants took this exercise with similar results they became very upset. They prided themselves on their uniformity and felt that the diversity of their responses to the word *dance* mocked their standardized procedures. In their words, "We're not dancers, we're accountants." They insisted that they be given a word that had something to do with their work, and that they would then produce greater commonality. When they were given the word *money,* however, they had even less in common.

Everyone Dances Their Own Dance

Our associations are unique. Accountants, artists, teachers, carpenters, secretaries, doctors, lawyers, and Cajun chefs—we are each unique. Each of us, as a result of heredity combined with individual experience, construes the world in our own special way. We are gifted, from the moment of birth with a special ability to experience and express the wonder of being alive. There is no one else like you, no one who can think and create as you do.

This diversity is not an accident. It's a critically important part of the evolutionary process that helps ensure the survival of the species. Given any type of adverse circumstance that may befall humanity, there is almost certainly someone with the special ability to overcome the challenge and carry on.

My colleague, Tony Buzan, writes and speaks poetically about human uniqueness. He cites the terms used to describe a fine diamond, ruby, or emerald:

> Jewels
> Gems
> Rarities
> Treasures
> Irreplaceable
> Precious

Buzan proclaims that every human being is immeasurably more precious, rare, and irreplaceable than the most beautiful stone imaginable.

Statisticians estimate that since the time of the first human, more than 70 billion of us have come and gone. If a super time-traveling photographer could take one giant photo of everyone who had ever existed you would still stand alone as one of a kind.

Each of us is an entire world.
—the Talmud

A Dance with Infinite Steps

Just as our associations are unique, they also are potentially unlimited. Our minds are capable of linking any thought with any other thought. If you doubt this, try to find a word that cannot be linked to the word *dance*. No matter how hard you search for an unrelatable word, you'll find that your mind can ultimately relate anything to anything else.

The exercise of finding unrelatable words is particularly fun when framed as a competition. For example, in one group a somewhat arrogant gentleman triumphantly challenged the rest of the class to link the word *antidisestablismentarianism* to *dance*. An erudite classmate pointed out that the word meant "opposition to the disestablishment of orthodox churches" who opposed, among other things, the practice of dancing. Someone else mentioned that *"antidisestablishmentarianism"* actually contains the letters of the french word for dance, *danse*. And, another person suggested that you can automatically connect this or any other strange word with *dance* as a member of that class of words you don't normally associate with *dance*.

These two simple truths—that our associations are *unique* and *unlimited*—have profound implications for communication and creative thinking. The first and most striking implication is that **the potential for misunderstanding in any communication is unlimited.** My mind is capable of making an unlimited number of associations with every single word that you say, and if your way of saying things and my way of hearing things is unique to each of us, it begins to seem amazing that we can communicate at all.

Misunderstanding is frequently the result not of orneriness or lack of consideration, but of associational difference. Our interpretation of events, and therefore our behavior, always tends to be consistent with our underlying patterns of association or "models of the world." These models are different for everyone, and they are all incomplete. We are all subject to believing the seductive notion that *our* world is *the* world.

This realization brings a much greater appreciation of the challenge of communication, and the difficulty and delicacy of fine-tuning your message to mesh with the associational nuances of another's unique world.

How many times have you had the experience of carefully explaining something to someone, watching him nod in apparent understanding, and then he does something entirely different from what you thought you'd agreed to? Much communication in organizations and personal relationships resembles the children's game of Telephone, in which a group of youngsters pass a "secret message"—a word or phrase—down the line, child to child. The result is totally unlike the original message.

Another powerful implication of this information is that **the only way to measure the results of your communication is with the response you get from your audience.**

We may feel that we are brilliantly articulate and persuasive, and that we cover all the points we wish to make. But the effectiveness of any kind of communication, from technical instructions to words of endearment, is always ultimately a function of the associational network of the person receiving the message. In other words, we can't know the success of our communication unless we monitor the actual response of our listeners.

Style-Flex

Another key to understanding and communicating effectively with others is the study of patterns or tendencies of association. Personality, cognitive, and learning theories posit many different ways of categorizing and predicting human behavior.

In a previous chapter, we introduced some of the differences between left- and right-brain types. This left/right typology also has significant implications for communication. If you are right-brain dominant, for example, and want to communicate with a left-brained group, you won't get very far if you begin by urging them to "see the big picture." And if you are a left-brainer attempting to communicate with more right-brain-oriented individuals, you won't get through to them by presenting reams of facts and data. Rather, you'll have to capture their imagination first.

Clients often say that their people are desperate for creativity, innovation, and new ways of perceiving and thinking, but they are afraid I won't be able to get through to them because they are so strongly left-brain dominant. A training director for a major chemical company once cautioned me that the R&D people attending an upcoming seminar "had their right hemispheres surgically removed."

If I were to come to these groups and start right in with mind mapping and imagination exercises, I'd alienate a large percentage of the audience. Instead, I begin with exercises that ground them in practical experience, presenting plenty of research and references to build a step-by-step, logical case for the power, value, and practical application of intuition, imagination, and synvergent thinking in work and personal life.

The left-right brain model is a simple tool that can be useful in understanding people. Another valuable "typology" for understanding oneself and others is the VAK: visual, auditory, kinesthetic model of learning-style preferences.

Visual, Auditory, Kinesthetic: the most effective communicators use all modes as the situation requires.

Individuals tend to process information according to three basic perceptual styles. Visual types think in visual terms—they prefer reading and visualizing. They often express this tendency through the use of linguistic references such as: "Do you *see* what I mean?" "Do we have a shared *picture* here?" "Yes, it's becoming *clear* to me." "That *looks* good."

Auditory types generally operate through their sense of hearing—they prefer to speak and listen. They employ such references as: "That *sounds* good to me." "I *hear* what you're saying." "Yes, that *rings* true." "I'm not sure I appreciate the *tone* of your remarks."

Kinesthetic types approach things through a sense of the body—they prefer to touch. They use phrases such as: "I can *grasp* your point." "I get a *feel* for what you're saying." "I can really get *hold* of that information." "I've got a *handle* on that."

One can imagine a Babel-like phenomenon if these three types tried to communicate.

> Visual: "Do you see what I mean? Do we have a shared vision here?"
>
> Kinesthetic: "I don't know, I can't quite grasp it. It just doesn't feel right."
>
> Auditory: "It doesn't ring a bell for me at all."

I tend to be more auditory than my wife, Nusa, who is strongly visual. In the courting phase of our relationship, I frequently offered verbal expressions of affection that were always pleasantly received but didn't have the impact I would have liked. Eventually, it dawned on me that, as a strongly visual type, she wanted it in writing. Cards, letters, and poems were the key. To be effective in communicating my message, I had to link with her preferred style of receiving it.

If you've ever had a boss who just wants to "see it in writing," you're probably dealing with a visual type. Visual types doodle a lot, and tend to speak a little more quickly than both auditory and kinesthetic types. Other visual verbal references include taking a dim view, in the light of, a bird's-eye view.

Kinesthetic types pace while thinking. They gesture more frequently and generally find it hard to sit still. They are hands-on people. If you have a colleague who always wants to "walk you through the process," you're probably dealing with a kinesthetic type. Other kinesthetic verbal references include come to grips with, hang in there, get in touch with. . . .

Auditory types will buy books on tape rather than read. They are happy to hold meetings on the telephone. Other auditory verbal references are it is unheard of, I hear you loud and clear, let me sound him out.

The most effective communicators among leaders, managers, parents, husbands, wives, teachers, and therapists combine all three modes fluidly.

Other widely employed typologies range from the Myers Briggs Type Indicator and the Wilson Learning Model of Managerial Styles to the Enneagram Personality Profile and Astrological Charting. Some are more scientific and reliable than others, but they all create a certain fascination—a promise of better understanding ourselves and others.

Typologies, generalizations, and categorizations can be useful predictors of behavioral tendencies. Yet there is a critical difference between typing and stereotyping. To refer to someone as a visual type, female, left-brain, extrovert, expressive-driver, scorpio—all offer information that can be useful in understanding and predicting some of people's actions. Yet, all too often, the generalizations we make obscure our awareness of each person's uniqueness. And, each of us is one of a kind, distinct from all others, even those who share many of the same categories.

The value of various typologies such as left-right brain, VAK, and Myers Briggs is, first of all, as tools for self understanding. They can serve as signposts on the path toward the development of wholeness and flexibility, increasing your awareness of the filters through which you see the world and allowing you to bring automatic patterns of response to consciousness. As you develop an understanding of your tendencies and proclivities, your strengths and weaknesses, you will experience a corresponding expansion of your ability to understand others.

Depending on the circumstance, you should be hard as a diamond, flexible as a willow, smooth-flowing like water, or as empty as space.
—*Morihei Ueshiba, master and aikido founder on "style-flex"*

As your insight into different types expands, so does your freedom to practice style-flex—the ability to use all modes as the situation requires. As you cultivate the talent for using *all* the colors on your palette you take a significant step on the path of personal growth and strengthen your leadership skill. And, you can raise this skill to a higher level by dedicating yourself to develop an ever-deepening understanding of the styles and tendencies of the individuals in your family and organization, supporting them in developing greater flexibility and wholeness.

Our planet is currently home to 6 billion unique individuals. Each one is a precious jewel unlike any other. At the same time, everyone is fundamentally the same in his and her humanness. We all desire to be seen, respected, and loved for our uniqueness. Cultivate your capacity to bear these two truths in your mind and heart by practicing the art of synvergent listening.

The Art of Synvergent Listening

Communication is life's most valuable skill. Leadership, whether at home or at work, is largely a function of the art of communication, and listening is the soul of communication. The art of listening is based on a commitment to understanding others. Webster defines understanding as "the power or ability to think and learn; intelligence; judgment; sense." To listen is "to make a conscious effort to hear."

Take an approach to listening that goes beyond just hearing, but follows Webster in emphasizing the importance of *conscious* effort. Without a conscious effort to listen and understand, we simply react to others, judging or following preconceived notions that ultimately interfere with our effectiveness. Instead of getting to know people, we project stereotypes we already hold.

Practice looking at the world from other people's points of view, not just intellectually but emotionally and spiritually as well. Suspend your belief that the world you perceive and understand is *the* world. Recognize that each person has his or her own special way of constructing things. Aspire to enter deeply into the perspective of the people in *your* world.

In most interactions, our repto-mammalian brain instantly makes a number of judgments such as Is this person friend or foe? What is this person's status in relation to mine? Although you can't prevent your fundamental programming from making these instant assessments, you can choose to *act* from the higher centers of your brain.

This quality of action is beautifully expressed in the prayer of St. Francis of Assisi:

Lord make me an instrument of your peace.
Where there is hatred, let me sow love
Where there is injury, pardon
Where there is doubt, faith,
Where there is despair, hope;
Where there is darkness, light; and
Where there is sadness, Joy;
O Divine Master, grant that I may not so much seek to be consoled as to
    console;
To be understood as to understand,
To be loved as to love
For it is in giving that we receive, it is in pardoning that we are pardoned
And it is in dying that we are born to eternal life.

St. Francis's inspiring words offer a powerful spiritual sentiment. But the idea of seeking primarily to love and understand is not just a matter of Sunday school philosophy. It is a practical key to everyday success with people.

Understanding *first* has a transformational power at work and at home, as the following examples illustrate.

In his efforts to create a more synergetic, team-oriented culture, the president of a leading broadcasting company aimed to improve communication between the news staff and the rest of the organization. Interviews around the company made it clear that although respect for the quality of their work was high, the news group was generally perceived as arrogant and unappreciative. For their part, the news group felt that the support they received did not always optimize their performance and that the rest of the organization did not understand or appreciate the urgency, pressure, and high-stakes nature of their day-to-day functioning. In a meeting with key news managers I led the group through an exercise in viewing the world from the perspective of the rest of the organization. I shared St. Francis's practical philosophy and urged them to "seek first to understand." The group seemed to realize the potency of this approach and decided to send emissaries out to other parts of the company to listen first and learn how to be more responsive. The result: other groups were amazed and inspired by the unprecedented concern for *their* problems. Their sense of being recognized and valued for their contributions grew and they redoubled their effectiveness in supporting the news team's mission.

The Franciscan approach gets results and if it can work for a group of tough-minded journalists it can work for anyone. One of the grizzled, veteran newsmen did come up after this session to remind me, "You know, I appreciate everything you said about St. Francis and all, but don't forget, he worked mostly with animals!"

The owner of an innovative restaurant chain faced a serious crisis shortly after launching his business. An idealist, he aspired to create a superior quality experience for his customers, predicated on a positive, people-oriented working environment. Despite Herculean efforts to set the stage for a positive culture, he was plagued by high management turnover and low morale. He had made the mistake of setting expectations so high that they could not be fulfilled.

Committed to transforming the situation, he authorized a company-wide attitude survey, with in-depth interviews. Afterward, he held a series of meetings with the entire organization. In each meeting he personally addressed every concern raised by his staff. He expressed a sincere understanding of people's frustrations, and offered an action plan to apply many of their suggestions. He spoke honestly about the suggestions he did not intend to implement.

The results were remarkable—a turnaround in morale with turnover dropping dramatically. One of the associates commented, "Everyone is just totally blown away by the fact that senior management actually listened and seems to understand."

In my own personal relationship, my wife, Nusa, is usually the most delightful, intelligent, and inspiring person to be around. That's why I married her. Yet, every now and then, I'll come home and find her irritable, snapping at me for what seems like no reason. I'm ready to react angrily, but instead I get smart and figure it out. I ask, "Sweetheart, is it that time?" She says yes. I go over and give her a hug. For the next couple of days, whenever there's a potential clash, I find that just understanding her circumstances makes it much easier to be compassionate and supportive. And, she tells me that whenever I am irrational and edgy, she pretends I have PMS, which makes it much easier to be compassionate and accepting of me.

BAD LISTENING

To develop your listening skills further you can pull the tail of the become-a-better-listener problem. Try this listening exercise with a partner. List all the manifestations of bad listening you encounter in the average week. Your list might read something like this:

- Skeptical facial expressions
- Finishing my sentences
- Overaffirming—"uh-huh, uh-huh, uh-huh"
- Stereotyping—"That's a typical (female, male, marketing, finance, liberal, conservative, etc.) perspective"
- Looking at his watch
- Answering the phone
- Constant fidgeting
- Interrupting
- Changing the subject
- Continual self-referencing ("Oh yeah, the same thing happens to *me* all the time" or the classic "Well, enough about me, I'd like to hear from you; what do you think about me!")
- Giving unwanted advice

- Failure to make eye contact
- Gooey, invasive overly sincere eye contact
- Leaving the room ("Please just carry on with what you're saying, I'll be back in a minute")
- Falling asleep

Now, tell your partner a real-life story, something meaningful that you'd really like to share. Your partner's job is to practice bad listening—to manifest as many of the nonaffirming listening habits as possible. Your task is to persist in communicating your message. After a minute or so, switch roles.

When this exercise is practiced in a class setting, the results are always fascinating. Tension quickly fills the room, often manifested in near-hysterical laughter. Even though everyone knows it's only a game, a real fight could break out if the exercise is allowed to continue for more than two or three minutes.

Clearly, bad listening can be painful for everyone concerned.

The first phase of this exercise sets the stage for a deeper consideration of listening. Before completing the exercise—when you and your partner truly listen to each other tell these same stories—consider the elements of this powerful leadership art.

Time, Place, and Relationship

An important prerequisite to listening well is an awareness of timing, place, and relationship. Under some circumstances, such as when you're distressed or preoccupied about something, genuine listening may be next to impossible. Sometimes it's best to say, "I can't talk to you now," and set a time and place where it is possible. Trying to listen, when you really can't, does not work. People usually sense when you are not truly with them.

It's also important to consider relationship. Your decision whether to listen carefully will be different when your child or spouse says, "I need to talk to you," than when a telemarketer tries to sell you something.

Real listening begins with commitment. Form a conscious intention to act consciously. Often this is difficult. We feel pulled in many directions, and our full attention isn't always available. In order to be in touch with someone else you must first be in touch with yourself. So the first step in the art of listening is to "center" yourself.

Find your center by becoming aware of the flow of your breathing. Do this for thirty seconds. By bringing your attention to your breath, you enter fully into the present moment (your breathing is always happening, "now"). Now you can look and listen with fresh eyes and an open mind. Suspend judgments and preconceptions. Focus your mind, soften your belly, open your heart, attune your spirit.

Put yourself into the other person's world. Be prepared to walk around in their shoes. This is not just an intellectual exercise. It's an emotional and spiritual one, too.

Empathy and the Paradox of Influence

Skilled listeners are empathic. The word *empathy* means to enter into the feeling of another's experience. It comes from the Greek root *empathia,* meaning "affection; passion." All the great religions preach love. This may seem like too grand an idea to translate into daily life, but the art of listening is a simple, everyday way to integrate this most noble of sentiments into actual practice.

We think of listening as an aural phenomenon. But the synvergent listener knows that listening is also a function of observation. Listen with your eyes. Open yourself to the messages communicated through people's body language. Bring your attention to the subtleties of facial expression. Look at their eyes and ask yourself, "What is the real message?" The eyes are a direct extension of the brain, the windows of the soul. They tell you what someone is really attempting to communicate.

Listen carefully to the quality of their voice tone. It is rich with meaning. Consider how much you can determine about a friend's emotional state from the way he or she says hello over the telephone.

Of course you also want to listen to the words. Listen so that you can repeat, in your own words, the content of the person's message. Usually, people are quite good at repeating back the content of a conversation. It's much harder to reflect back the essence. Be prepared to repeat the words *and reflect the feeling and spirit* of the person to whom you are listening.

The idealistic restaurant owner referred to earlier in this chapter was successful in transforming his culture because he combined accurate repetition of his staff's feedback with empathic reflection of their emotions. One of the biggest challenges to doing this appears when you disagree with the other person's point of view.

It's easy to be an empathic listener when you have no problem with what the person is saying. The real challenge comes when there is disagreement and conflict. The key is to remember that *understanding does not necessarily imply agreement*. If you are serious about listening, be willing to repeat the content and reflect the essence, to the satisfaction of the person with whom you're communicating. In other words, you withhold the expression of your own opinions until the other person agrees that you have understood their point of view. This is a transformational key to interpersonal problem solving, negotiation, and conflict resolution.

Listening is one of the most powerful forms of communicating. By listening, you communicate to others the depth of your concern and care. Listening is an act of leadership. It takes courage. As Stephen Covey emphasizes: "It takes a great deal of security to go deep into a listening experience because you open yourself up to be influenced. . . . It's a paradox . . . because in order to have influence, you have to be influenced." The more you allow yourself to be open to others, the greater your ability to influence them.

Listening would be a lot easier if each of us were in touch with our own feelings and able to articulate them freely. Frequently, people do not seem to know what they mean, and they have a difficult time expressing themselves. Nevertheless, the emotional context of rapport that you create by listening in an empathic way serves as a framework to help people discover what they really need to communicate.

Love is the only way to grasp another human being . . . to see the essential traits and features . . . [the] potential in him which is not yet actualized but ought to be actualized . . . by his love, the loving person enables the beloved person to actualize these potentialities.
—Viktor Frankl

In colloquial language, we speak about putting ourselves in some-one else's position. Some guides to listening actually teach this as a technique. They encourage you to assume the posture of the person to whom you're listening as a way to establish rapport. It's much more effective, however, to really open yourself to the feeling of rapport. Your body language will then naturally align with the speakers.

True empathic listening is a rare experience. In a study of different systems of psychotherapy, researchers found that whatever the psy-chotherapeutic style, one-third of the patients seemed to improve, one-third stayed the same, and one-third got worse. Of those who im-proved, the patients experienced one key ingredient in common: **ac-curate empathy.** Sadly, the only time many of us have the experience of accurate empathy is when we pay for it in therapy. Even then, we have only a one-in-three chance of finding it.

Most people experience only very rare moments of being understood by another. Frequently, this fleeting experience becomes the basis for falling in love. In a world where people see stereotypes and can't slow down to recognize the soul of another being, the simple act of empathic listening can have a profoundly positive effect.

The art of listening is a synvergent activity requiring understanding of the paradox of influence and the use of both sides of the brain. We listen for content and facts, with our left brain, and we listen for feel-ing, body language, voice tonality, and gestalt with our right.

Each of us is an irreplaceable gem, unlike any other. We are, at the same time, fundamentally the same. We all long to be seen, respected, and appreciated in our uniqueness. As you hold these two truths in your mind and heart you'll be better able to listen, build trust, and get results.

Mind Mapping for Better Communication

Mind mapping can help you improve your listening and communica-tion skills in a number of powerful ways:

- **Practice proactive listening**
- **Conflict resolution: see the other point of view**

- **Negotiation: invent options for mutual gain**
- **Plan and conduct memorable meetings**
- **Plan and record telephone calls**

PRACTICE PROACTIVE LISTENING

Cultivate your empathic capabilities by using mind maps to help you practice proactive listening. Proactive listening involves *practicing* looking at the world from someone else's perspective. Contemplate the worldview or "associational patterning" of your spouse, child, customer, client, boss, or co-worker. You can do this by using your imagination to become this person. Imagine that you came from their background and lived inside their body. Then, make a mind map of their motivations, concerns, likes and dislikes, needs and worries. The purpose of this exercise is not to try to figure out the other person, but rather to focus your mind and heart more deeply.

The beginning of a proactive listening map.

When you have done this exercise for the different key individuals in your life, try doing one large "systems map" combining all of them;

each person becomes a major branch of your mind map. Synvergent thinkers know that the separate, independent individuals in an organization or a family are also interdependent aspects of a system. A system is "a set or arrangement . . . so related or connected as to form a unity or organic whole." In other words, what happens to one part affects all the others. As you gain insight into systems, your ability to understand and appreciate individuals, including yourself, grows exponentially.

CONFLICT RESOLUTION: USE MIND MAPS TO SEE THE OTHER POINT OF VIEW

The most challenging element in conflict resolution is getting people to appreciate the opposing point of view. Mind mapping makes it easier to look at something from someone else's perspective. For example, take the owner of a burgeoning restaurant chain who faced a conflict that threatened the growth of his business. Preparations for the opening of his second unit were disrupted by a dispute between the general managers of his original and new operations. The owner was at a loss. As he expressed it, "They are at each other's throats and it is poisoning the whole culture."

Motivated by the owner's threat to dismiss one or possibly both of them if they didn't resolve things promptly, the two agreed to meet and try to work it out. I asked them to prepare for the session by making a comprehensive mind map of their respective versions of what had gone wrong in their relationship.

We began the session by flipping a coin to see who would go first. The manager of the original store won the toss and started. We agreed that he would have fifteen minutes to give a guided tour of his mind map. His counterpart's task was to practice the art of listening—no comments, questions, fidgeting, or arguing allowed, just empathy. After the first fifteen minutes they reversed roles.

At the end of the second presentation, I asked them to reflect back the essence of the other's message. Then we had an open discussion. The first manager commented: "I never really saw your point of view before. This has opened my eyes." The second manager exclaimed, "This is the first time I've felt that you weren't out to get me."

The practice of just listening is powerful by itself, but the use of mind maps makes it even more effective. Mind mapping affords the participants the opportunity to *see,* in images, color, and key words, the other point of view.

In the case described above, a turning point came when the manager of the new store was presenting his case. He explained: "I feel that you just don't give me any respect. The very first time, we met you wouldn't look me in the eye and you shook my hand as though I didn't exist." His mind map included a traced outline of a hand and two out-of-focus eyes with a big red line drawn through the center. His counterpart later told me: "When I saw that [mind map], I knew he wasn't just making this stuff up."

Having established some understanding and rapport, I asked them each to mind map and present their recommendations for improving cooperation and team synergy between their respective staffs. They reached a number of important agreements, agreed to disagree on a few things, and finished with strong eye contact and a firm handshake. Although they have yet to become friends, they were able to work together to launch what is now a thriving chain.

If you want to influence them, you also need to understand . . . the power of their point of view and to feel the emotional force with which they believe it. It is not enough to study them like beetles under a microscope; you need to know what it feels like to be a beetle.
—*Fisher and Ury in* Getting To Yes

NEGOTIATE: INVENT OPTIONS FOR MUTUAL GAIN

An advertisement for a popular negotiation seminar states, "In business, you don't get what you deserve, you get what you negotiate!" The same can be said of life in general. In their classic bestseller, *Getting To Yes,* Roger Fisher and William Ury emphasize that with empathy for the opposing point of view as a point of departure, the best negotiators succeed by "inventing options for mutual gain." They stress that the process of generating a wide range of possible solutions opens up the "room for negotiation" and makes a positive resolution much more likely. This creative approach frequently results in a win/win solution that exceeds both parties' original expectations.

If you apply mind mapping and the skills of creative problem solving, your ability to generate win/win solutions will flower dramatically. As a senior partner of a Wall Street investment firm wrote after attending a mind mapping/synvergent thinking seminar, "We are presently engaged in a most important, to us at least, litigation in Chicago. As in all litigations we are at the stage where settlement is within the realm of possibility without actual trial. In order to prepare for settlement negotiations, one really must try and think the problem through, both from your own point of view and that of your opponents. I found that by making a mind map of the problem (and then sleeping on it overnight) a solution, at least one that appealed to me and seems logical, absolutely popped out of the page."

PLAN AND CONDUCT MEMORABLE MEETINGS

Meetings top the charts in surveys of organizational time wasters. Mind mapping can help you plan, conduct, and remember more efficient, effective, and enjoyable meetings. To plan great meetings, begin by mind mapping the seven P's: purpose, place, people, pace, preparation, program, and process.

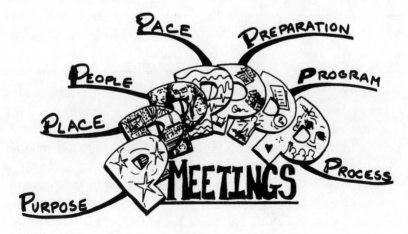

Seven "Ps" for **P**owerful meetings.

- *Purpose:* What, specifically, would you like the meeting to accomplish?
- *Place:* Create a brain-nourishing environment. Set up chairs and tables to suit your purpose. For a refreshing approach to brief meetings, remove all the chairs and conduct the meeting standing up.
- *People:* Who needs to attend, who doesn't? If possible, invite people with diverse, complementary thinking styles.
- *Pace:* Set a specific start time and honor it. Keep things moving. Focus on key information and slice through baloney. If a meeting isn't energizing it's not worth having.
- *Preparation:* Is there anything that people should read, discuss, or think about before they come?
- *Program:* Your program should always reflect your purpose. Plan the agenda carefully and then *be prepared to improvise* if the quest to meet your objectives suggests a different course. Cultivate the art of distinguishing the fine line between new pathways of creative association and meaningless, tangential rambling.
- *Process:* The process for running your meetings will vary, depending on your purpose, but there are a few principles and practices that apply universally:

If your group is just beginning to work together, *bring in a trained facilitator*. As your group matures, encourage all the members to develop meeting management skills by assigning the facilitation role internally on a rotating basis. After facing the challenge of guiding meetings themselves, people become more sensitive to the flow of the meeting process. As each person's sensitivity grows, a positive group intelligence emerges and meetings start to become self-regulating, synergetic events.

Encourage participation and empathic listening. Try asking each person, in turn, to speak for a set time, perhaps two to five minutes, while the group practices the art of listening.

Take brain breaks. Many old paradigm managers treat meeting duration as a badge of courage. Their perverse pride in bladder control does not correlate with effectiveness. Take a five- or ten-minute break every forty-five to ninety minutes and you will get *more* high-quality work done.

Use mind mapping to record and reflect each participant's contribution. Cover the walls with giant sheets of blank paper or use multiple flip charts. Assign a scribe to map each person's remarks. In smaller meetings (fewer than seven people), assign a color to each participant. This makes it easy to track participation and see the relationships between the ideas expressed. If your emerging mind map is primarily green, red, black, and orange you might ask "blue," "brown," and "purple" to add their comments. The free-flowing structure of the mind map encourages participation and creative association. At the same time, mind mapping ideas also shifts the emphasis from who said what to what was said, making meetings less ego centered and more idea centered.

In addition to its effectiveness in planning and conducting your meeting, you can use mind mapping to preserve and remember the fruits of your labor. As the members of your work team become "mind map literate," capture the minutes of meetings in mind map form.

PLAN AND RECORD TELEPHONE CALLS

Have you ever had the embarrassing and potentially expensive experience of hanging up the telephone and suddenly remembering something you forgot to mention? This happens because as you talk, your mind generates associations. When you hang up, the association process continues, often yielding important insight. You can speed the process of association and improve your effectiveness over the phone by mind mapping your thoughts for a call before you make it. In addition to helping you plan your calls, you can also make mind maps as you speak, recording key points made by the other party and generating and organizing your own creative responses in process.

Characteristics of Great Communicators

If you remember that the only way to measure the success of a communication is by the response that it generates and that there is an unlimited possibility for misunderstanding in every communication you will be well on your way to greater effectiveness as a communicator. And, as you apply the skills of style-flex, synvergent listening, and mind mapping, you will discover that others start appreciating and listening to you in a new way; they will begin looking to you for leadership. What are some of the other characteristics of the most effective communicators and leaders and how can you become one?

TAKE 100 PERCENT RESPONSIBILITY

Taking 100 percent responsibility doesn't mean that you "create your own reality." Regardless of your way of thinking, you will find that if you lie down on a busy highway you will soon have a flat and squishy reality. You do, however, affect your reality dramatically by your choice of response.

We must be the change we wish to see in the world.
—Gandhi

The usual assumption people bring to communication is that responsibility for it is shared equally, fifty-fifty. The most effective communicators make a different assumption. They act as though they are 100 percent responsible for:

- Accurately understanding others
- Getting their message across to them
- Whatever is achieved as a result

At the other extreme, whiners act like everything is someone else's fault. To assess and nurture your response-ability, monitor your attitudes as they are reflected in your language and rate yourself on the continuum from whiner to high performer.

Classic lines from the lower end of the continuum include:

"If I've told you once I've told you a thousand times"
"My wife doesn't understand me"
"I can't get anyone at work to listen"
"If only . . ."

"I can't"
"There's nothing we can do about it"
"*They* won't let me"
"He *makes* me furious"

If you catch yourself indulging in any of the above or any other form of whining, blaming, complaining, and commiserating ("being miserable together"), do not attempt to change directly. Instead of grafting superficial "positive self-talk" on top of your current real feelings just observe or "witness" the whining behavior. The difference is that now, you are conscious, so you are free to *choose* to whine! Of course, once you are awake, whining starts to get a little boring, so have some fun exaggerating the whining, blaming, complaining, or commiserating. (Take a few minutes and whine aloud: WAAAAAAH, WAAAAAAAH, WAAAAAAAAAAH in the most nasal tones you can manage—this is a fun exercise to try with others. Have a competition to see who can create the most annoying whine; or, try a commiseration contest: "When I was growing up we had to walk five miles to school *in the snow.*" "Oh yeah, that's nothing. When I was growing up we had to walk ten miles to school *in our bare feet.*" "You guys had it easy. When I was growing up we had to walk twenty miles to school and *we didn't have feet!*")

Would you care for some cheese with that whine?
—Anon

Once you have acknowledged, accepted, and chuckled about the part of you that loves to whine you are able to choose a more constructive orientation. Some reflections from the higher end of the continuum include:

I am choosing my response to this person.
I teach people how to treat me.
I can only change others by changing the way I see them.
How can I alter my approach to generate better results?
Let's find a way to work together to make it happen.

How does what I detest about this person mirror something in my own character?

In the happiest relationships and most effective organizations *everyone* takes 100 percent resposibility for successful communication.

Everything can be taken from a man but one thing: the last of the human freedoms—to choose one's attitude in any given set of circumstances.
—Viktor Frankl

TAKE A SYNVERGENT PERSPECTIVE ON HUMAN NATURE AND PRACTICE CONSCIOUS OPTIMISM

Are people fundamentally good or bad? Are we angels incarnate or vicious animals? Are you a fan of Hobbes or Rousseau? Much of our political history in the West can be understood as a struggle between these two philosophies of human nature. Well, get ready for a blinding flash of what should now be obvious—they are both right. And, the "mental sets" you adopt regarding people's fundamental nature influence their behavior toward you. Numerous studies in academic, military, and corporate situations reveal that the expectations of a teacher, drill sergeant, or boss affect performance significantly: positive expectations yield better performance; with negative expectations, performance declines. In other words, if you believe that people can't be trusted, you will probably find yourself surrounded by untrustworthy people. Moreover, people will not trust you either, since your philosophy of human nature obviously must apply to yourself as well!

So, philosophies aside, bring out the best in others, and yourself, by expecting nothing less.

NURTURE COOPERATION, TEAMWORK AND CREATIVE COMPETITION

Over the years I've worked in many organizations filled with well-educated, intelligent people. Although pressures abound, most of these organizations are, by any objective measurement, remarkably affluent.

Yet, some are miserable rat holes pervaded by fear and others are fun, inspiring places to be. What is the difference? It is best summed up in the parable of the banquet table.

Heaven and hell are the same. In each place people sit at large rectangular banquet tables. The tables are set beautifully and replete with every imaginable delicacy. All the diners in both settings have large wooden paddles strapped to their hands, and the paddles can't be removed. In hell everyone tries to feed themselves, food flies in all directions, and fights break out constantly. In heaven everyone feeds the person across from them at the table.

In the movie *GlenGarry, GlenRoss,* Alec Baldwin plays the head of sales for a cheesy real estate company. His motivational strategy is straight from hell. Aiming to spur his team on he announces a sales competition—"First prize is a new Cadillac, second prize is a set of steak knives, third prize is you're fired."

The best communicators, motivators, and leaders take a different approach. They view competition in accordance with the original Olympic ideal: A javelin thrower throws his best to honor the gods, expressing the glory of humanity, and inspiring his opponent to greater achievement. The opponent responds by mustering his best aiming to spur his competitor to further glory. Competition becomes a creative process, energizing the never-ending quest for excellence.

Leaders know that the "com" in communicate means "together." They nurture teamwork, cooperation, and creative competition by identifying and then reminding people of their common interests and ideals. They seek to bring out the best in others by seeing them accurately, appealing to their strengths, and supporting their areas of growth. They leverage diversity by orchestrating teams based on complementary tendencies and styles. And they consistently recognize and reward teamwork.

BE HONEST WITHOUT BEING NAIVE

Many organizations make false promises to live by lofty codes of values created by consultants or the senior team on a weekend retreat. They would be better off if they just told people, "Look, you're lucky to have a job! You aren't here to have a meaningful experience. Now get back to work." At least the *honesty* of that approach would let people know where they stand, and they wouldn't waste time and energy on illusions.

Many members of the corporate workforce are like the middle-class members of psychiatrist Rollo May's study of abused children. Dr. May followed the lives of these children into adulthood and measured their baseline level of anxiety. He discovered a striking difference in the anxiety levels between the working-class and the middle-class subjects.

The middle-class people had much higher levels of anxiety. May attributes this to their having been lied to as children. Their parents, while denying their own hostility and abusive behavior, had promised them good lives and held high expectations for them. The working-class group also had been treated poorly, but they were not subjected to any false promises. May concluded that prolonged exposure to this type of illusion causes disability in knowing one's world, leading to a deep sense of alienation, confusion, and anxiety.

It is difficult, but essential, to be honest with oneself and others, especially in times of rapid change. When things are changing fast there is always an information crisis: either a shortage of essential information and/or an overload of false and misleading information. Everyone tends to assume that "*they* aren't really telling us what is going on." Frequently, "they" have no idea! Sometimes, "they" do know, but the timing for sharing the information is wrong for legitimate reasons. In any case, if you are "they," honesty is the best policy. Be accessible and share what you can in a timely and open manner. Information gaps are almost always filled by rumor and gossip. When necessary, learn to say either "I don't know" (with authority) or "I am not going to tell you now" (with empathy). Honesty doesn't mean blurting out everything at any old time just because it happens to be true. As Dr. Johnson once said, "Honesty is not greater where elegance is less."

Act with Integrity and Humility. Acting with integrity requires doing what you say you are going to do. Many people view this issue in a context of morality and righteousness, but for a fresh perspective let's consider it from the vantage point of recent brain research. When people fail to act with integrity it is usually because they are not integrated. Our greatest self-delusion is the belief that we are one inte-grated consciousness; that when we say "I" we are always talking about the same personality. As Dr. Robert Ornstein of the University of Cal-ifornia Medical Center and author of *The Evolution of Conscious-ness* emphasizes, "Our natural view of our mental state is deeply distorted . . . the oneness we feel is an illusion . . . we are not the same person from day to day or moment to moment. Our mind contains a special system, hidden from our view, that quietly preserves the illu-sion of unity." In other words, the difference between you and me and "Sybil" is not one of kind, but of degree.

To have integrity we must be honest about the fact that we are not integrated. That we don't always do what we say we will do. So, de-veloping integrity requires more than just good intentions. It demands increasing consciousness, openness to feedback and humility, mani-festing in the willingness to apologize and make amends when appro-priate.

PROMISE LOW AND DELIVER HIGH

Smart people with integrity promise low and aim to deliver high. Fools promise high and deliver low. For example, if you call a meeting and promise people that it will be over by 4:00 and you keep them until 4:30; you will not only lose some respect but you will also have a lousy meeting. You will get much better results if you tell people to plan to stay until 5:00 and that you will try to get them out earlier. Then, when the meeting ends at 4:45, you're a hero.

MANIFEST BASIC GOODNESS

Cynics believe that "nice guys finish last" but they forget that "the win-ner of the rat race is still a rat." The best leaders I've ever met are tough, street-smart, highly competitive and decent, kind and generous. They are idealistic realists and realistic idealists. Cynics may say, "He who has the gold rules," but the best leaders really do live by the golden rule. About twenty years ago I had an experience right out of a *New Yorker* cartoon that emphasized this point. As an enthusiastic seeker of esoteric truths I received word that a renowned Naqshabandi Sufi master was coming to town to teach. Although the event was not publicized, I managed to discover the time and place and traveled to an obscure location way across town. There was a considerable turnout and the air was charged with vibrant expectation. After a period of prayer and meditation, the sheik appeared, resplendent in his turban and robe. I was on the edge of my prayer cushion waiting for pearls of esoteric insight, when the Sheik said, "Don't do bad, do good."

Take the sheik's counsel as your point of departure.

Intensify the Search for Authenticity as You Gain Power

It is hard to pick up a newspaper without reading about a powerful person who has been arrested for corruption. Why do so many people lose touch with "basic goodness" and become corrupt as they assume power? Character is like a vessel, power is like wine. As the vessel is filled with increasing amounts of wine the tiny cracks in it start to rupture. (Some people have obvious, gaping holes in their character; but everyone has these tiny cracks. People who claim to have perfect vessels are self-deluded or lying.) To avoid becoming drunk with power, leaders must deepen their commitment to personal growth. As you achieve success, nurture your consciousness, question your motivations, and seek objective, honest feedback. If you are surrounded by people who always agree with you, something is wrong. If you believe all of your own publicity, you are headed for a fall.

Decline to Participate in Gossip and Rumor

When I was in college I had a friend, Donna, who was also pals with my girlfriend, Marilyn. After Marilyn and I broke up, Donna seemed to be the obvious source for intelligence about Marilyn—did she still like me, who was she dating, the usual. But, Donna, displaying uncommon wisdom, wasn't talking. She explained that she kept confidences and wouldn't tell Marilyn anything about me either. Despite intense attempts at persuasion, I couldn't even get her to give me hints or clues. At first I was annoyed because I was keen for information, but soon I realized that Donna was smart. She maintained her friendship with both of us by keeping her mouth shut. The most effective communicators and leaders are like Donna. They build trust by resisting the temptation to indulge in gossip and rumor. When you participate or collude in gossip, you communicate a message that compromises your ability to lead: that you can't be trusted behind my back either.

Use Jargon Only in Context

Jargon, in the form of code words, phrases, or acronyms, can be an efficient way to communicate, and it can help teams build a sense of alignment through a shared special language. Of course, it's useful only if everyone involved understands it. It is amazing how frequently computer, financial, and automotive salespeople, just to name a few, use jargon that their potential customers don't understand. And, in many organizations, the engineers love to use jargon that the marketing department doesn't understand and marketing gets revenge by making up jargon that no one understands.

Use MAPS (Metaphors, Analogies, Parables, and Stories)

Aristotle wrote, "The greatest thing by far is to be a master of metaphor." Metaphors, analogies, parables, and stories link new learning to existing knowledge. They make complex ideas simple. MAPS appeal to the whole brain and are more memorable and inspiring than straight information. Of course, it's essential to use the right MAPS with the right person or group. Metaphors from the ballfield, the battleground, or the barnyard, for example, may delight some people while alienating others. Metaphors from nature, science, music, and transportation (ships, planes, etc.) will usually work with anyone.

The very best communicators build an internal library of metaphors, analogies, parables, and stories and delight in making up their own, and they avoid clichés. The writings of Shakespeare, Robert Fulghum, Dave Barry, Idries Shah, and the Bible provide treasure troves of vivifying MAPS.

MASTER THE ART OF FEEDBACK

The most effective leaders do more than just inspire people toward a vision, they guide the journey by offering constructive feedback. If you practice the art of synvergent listening you will lay the groundwork for giving great feedback. Like listening, feedback requires the ability to enter empathically into the world of another. Great feedback is:

Offered in a context of support—For your feedback to be taken to heart you must create and sustain an atmosphere of rapport, trust, and respect. Effective feedback is offered in the context of support and with the spirit of continuous improvement. It is most effective when solicited rather than imposed. If your feedback springs from empathic observation, sensitivity, respect, and a sincere concern to guide others to fulfill their highest potential then people will increasingly seek you out to ask for it.

Timely and well-timed—Feedback is most useful when given promptly. If you want to give someone feedback on his performance at a meeting, for example, give it as soon as possible after the meeting rather than a few weeks later. In addition to being timely you want to ensure that the feedback is *well-timed*. Sensitivity to receptiveness and emotional state is key. Ask, "Is this a good time for me to give you some feedback on your performance?" or "When can we get together for a feedback session?" The best feedback is useless if the time or place prevents it from being digested. For example, even the most brilliant critical feedback will almost always do more harm than good if offered in public.

Specific and descriptive—Specifics are more constructive than broad generalities, and descriptions of behavior are more useful than summary judgments. To tell someone: "You are insensitive to clients," or "You are a slob," is not as constructive as: "You interrupted the client twice and failed to make eye contact," or "Your shirt tail was hanging out and your shoes were unshined."

Actionable—To be useful, feedback must refer to a behavior that a person can change. To remind someone of something that he is powerless to change is only to increase his frustration and sabotage trust. For example, "John, I'm afraid that you just aren't tall enough to cut the right figure in sales meetings." Instead, "John, we have got to find a way to strengthen your presence in sales meetings."

Prefaced with a question—Before launching into a discourse on someone's performance it is a good idea to *ask* him to evaluate his strengths and weaknesses first. People are usually much more receptive to your observations when you demonstrate respect by asking for theirs. Moreover, by asking first, and listening carefully, you will usually learn something valuable that you would not have known otherwise.

Sharing relevant information and allowing people to draw their own conclusions instead of offering advice. When you tell someone what to do you compromise her freedom to decide for herself. Advice is appropriate when someone is truly stuck, the situation is a pressing priority or, it is specifically requested.

Focused on what *is said and done, not on* why. It is dangerous to assume that we know why someone does what she does. And it is usually disastrous to tell someone what she "really" means or is "actually" trying to accomplish. Most people react to an unsolicited analysis of their motivations or intent with defensiveness and resentment. Attend to the observable rather than the inferred. If you have lingering uncertainty about someone's motivation or intent then ask for clarification.

Generous with praise and recognition—Chances are that most people in your organization and family feel unappreciated. Research suggests that to be perceived as evenhanded you must give four positive comments for every negative. Catching someone doing something right and acknowledging him for it costs nothing, builds morale, and encourages confidence.

Honest and direct regarding areas for improvement—Although many people suffer from feedback that is overly critical, harsh, and judgmental it is equally common to err by trying to always be nice. Nonperformers are frequently coddled and given positive performance reviews because the manager in charge doesn't want to hurt anyone's feelings or take responsibility for writing an unsatisfactory evaluation. Paradoxically, being too nice is a grave insult. The underlying message is that the person is incapable of learning, growing, and improving his performance. Moreover, if you can't find areas of improvement for your people to work on then you shouldn't be a manager and you will never be a leader. Leaders have the guts to tell people the truth even when it isn't comfortable. When offering constructive feedback avoid sugarcoating or beating around the bush. Tell people when you are not satisfied with their performance and specifically why. Guide them to create a plan for change. Encourage them to do their best.

Checked—Complete your feedback session by asking the recipient to express what she has understood. Check that her response matches your associations with your original message.

Monitored—You know that the only way to measure the success of a communication is through the results you acheive with your audience. So, measure your effectiveness as a giver of feedback by the changes of behavior that you observe in its wake.

Sought by leaders—The finest leaders build trust and learn continuously by *asking for feedback themselves.* They are secure and confident enough to seek critical input from co-workers, customers, vendors, bosses, and family members. And, if you aim to master the art of feedback then ask for feedback on your feedback.

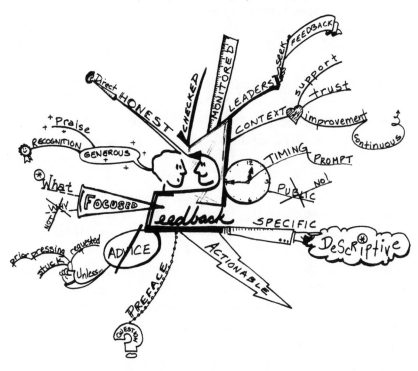

A mind map on the art of feedback.

GO ONE-ON-ONE

The most effective leaders understand that results are generated through relationships and that relationships are best cultivated one-on-one. People "do not care how much you know until they know how much you care," and investing the time to meet individually is one of the best ways to show that you care. Many misunderstandings in the workplace and at home can be traced to a failure of the individuals involved to take the time to sit down together and work it out. If you are a parent, set aside time to spend with each of your children. If you are a boss, take time, on a regular basis, to meet one-on-one with your team members, customers, and allies.

Paradoxically, the best speakers and presenters are those who can give every member of a vast audience the feeling that they are being addressed in a personal, even intimate, fashion. What are the secrets of the very best presenters and how can you become one? Read on.

—⊶⊷—

High Performance Presentations

Speak Synvergently

Most presentations in business and academic life are boring, handicapped by a convergent, left-brain imbalance. Managers, academics, and other professionals usually assemble facts and then present them in a detailed, exhaustive fashion. After a perfunctory "Good morning," little effort is made to establish rapport, and the only food for imagination is provided by the audience themselves through daydreaming and doodling.

Of course, your message must be convincing to the left brain. A great presentation is clear, concise, and compellingly *logical*. But logic alone is not enough. A great presentation *captures the audience's imagination* by speaking to the right brain. The elements of rhythm, color, timing, imagery, humor, dimension, and synthesis make facts come to life, enhancing the meaning and memorability of the message.

A great presentation requires another essential ingredient—establishing and maintaining *rapport* with your audience. Although rapport is influenced by both your logical and imaginative minds, it is primarily a function of emotional contact. And emotions are the province of the repto-mammalian brain. The repto-mammalian brain instinctively asks, "Is this person friend or foe?" As you deliver the first few minutes of your presentation, most of your audience already has unconsciously decided whether you are likable and if they are willing to be influenced by you.

Your credibility is not determined by the list of qualifications recited by the person who introduces you. Rather, it is created by the extent to which the audience perceives that you are authentically interested in communicating something of value to them. The synvergent approach to presentation offered in this chapter guides you to use your whole brain to reach the whole brain of your audience. This approach is based on the following assumptions:

1. Presentation skill is a key to leadership and long-term success.
Many well-educated, hardworking people have seen their careers stalled because they haven't developed the art of presentation. Others have risen to the top of their fields by cultivating this essential leadership skill.

A stock-market analyst was promoted to director of research of a multibillion-dollar pension fund in 1985, largely as a result of a series of presentations he gave on the status of various industries. His boss had asked the research group to put together eight presentations and he volunteered for the first one. When no one came forward to do the second one, he volunteered again. Same for all eight. Shortly afterward, he was promoted. In 1986, he was promoted to director of equity investments, and in 1990, he was elevated to a vice presidency and directorship of the entire fund. He attributes much of his success to his commitment to mastering the art of synvergent presentation:

> My devotion to continuous improvement of my communication and presentation skills is the principal differentiating factor between myself and my competition in my career on three levels: first, by basing all my presentations on careful listening and sensitivity to my clients needs I build their confidence and gain their trust; second, by disciplining myself to deliver a simple, clear message, I refine my own thinking so it is focused; and third, by communicating the message in a creative and entertaining fashion I ensure that my clients will not be able to forget it.

As the above story illustrates, leadership demands the ability to present at a high level. Former Chrysler chairman and business legend Lee Iacocca also attributes much of his success to his skill as a communicator: "I've seen a lot of guys who are smarter than I am and a lot who know more about cars. And yet I lost them in the smoke. Why? Because I'm tough? No. You don't succeed for very long by kicking people around. You have got to know how to talk to them, plain and simple."

Many technically competent individuals discover that their own personal Peter principle, or level of incompetence, is a function of a failure to inspire others. No matter how well educated or creative you are, you must be able to communicate your ideas effectively to have them implemented. Moreover, in the rapidly changing environment of the nanosecond nineties, speaking skills are more important than ever. Leaders must be able to inform and inspire to maintain alignment in times of chaos.

2. The discipline of presentation is a critical element in thinking. The process of preparing a simple, powerful expression of complex ideas forces you to clarify and refine your thoughts. You do not know what you are talking about unless you are able to articulate your message so that others can understand it.

3. You can learn to give great presentations. Many organizations offer courses with titles such as "Oral Presentations I" and "Presentation Skills." These courses tend to focus on teaching people to survive a presentation without embarrassing themselves. One popular manual calls for "ensuring a minimum standard of competence." This survival orientation results in boring and ineffective presentations.

Instead, approach the art of presenting with a mental set that focuses on excellence through continuous improvement. This attitude improves communication and encourages leadership. Paradoxically, the focus on giving great presentations becomes the key to transforming the fear that leads people to focus on just surviving.

Whether you are an extrovert, introvert, left- or right-brainer, presenting is a skill you can learn. More accurately, you can unlearn the habits you have developed that interfere with your natural brilliance as a communicator. When you were a baby, you were naturally expressive and totally engaging. You had charisma. If you release your natural abilities and cultivate an understanding of the path of excellence, you can become a first-class, superbaby presenter!

4. Authenticity is the source of authority. The word *authentic* comes from the roots *auto,* meaning "self," and *entea,* meaning "instrument" or "tool." Authentic means "genuine, original, trustworthy, reliable." The self is your original instrument for communication. Your credibility as a speaker and a leader is directly correlated with the extent to which the audience perceives that you are genuine. Your greatest effectiveness comes from being yourself. Who you are communicates more than what you say.

A reporter once asked Mahadev Desai, Gandhi's personal secretary, the secret of Gandhi's ability to enchant audiences for hours without using a script or notes. Desai replied, "What Gandhi thinks, what he feels, what he says, and what he does are all the same. He does not need notes." This is the power of inner alignment, of authenticity.

5. To grow as a presenter, you must grow as a person. In his classic, *On Becoming a Leader,* Warren Bennis emphasizes that the quest for authenticity is the heart of leadership. Presentations are a mirror that reflect your progress in this quest. To be a great presenter, you must learn to speak from your true self. In our society it is not always easy to know or to be yourself. The development of authenticity, and great presentation skill, is part of a lifelong process of personal growth.

6. Preparation is half the battle. Although fear of public speaking is a major factor in the mediocrity of many presentations, the real culprit often is lack of preparation. Why don't people prepare? Perhaps fear leads them to ignore or deny the whole subject until the last minute. Maybe it is a result of a habit of "cramming" developed through years of schooling. Some people don't prepare because they fail to recognize the importance of presentations. Others just don't think of themselves as presenters.

In a study conducted at a major oil company a team of psychologists attempted to distinguish the key differentiating characteristics of the most creative people in the company. After three months of intensive testing and interviewing, the researchers concluded that there was one critical difference: the highly creative people thought of themselves as such, the less creative people believed that they weren't creative.

The same is true for presenting. Poor presenters think of themselves that way. So they don't prepare. They don't look for opportunities to improve or practice. They aren't mentally set to discover stories, news items, and other information that could make their presentations more interesting and enjoyable. Conversely, the best presenters pride themselves on their communication skill. They take every opportunity to practice and improve. With their minds set on success, they are continuously researching, generating, incubating, and evaluating ideas to enrich their presentations.

7. Preparation plus authenticity = great presentations. The simple formula for giving great presentations is preparation plus authenticity. The most powerful presenters integrate a command of their subject with natural, authentic self-expression. Research, preparation, and practice set the stage for a confident, natural delivery. If you don't know your subject, you deserve to be nervous. On the other hand, you can't know everything. A powerful presenter and effective leader is able to say "I don't know" with authority!

To give great presentations do your homework, and be yourself.

So what are the specific elements of great presentations and how can you learn to give them? Try this. . . .

Target Your Message

The operation was a success, but the patient died.
—Anon

The success of your presentation can only be measured by the results you achieve with your audience. If you think of your audience as customers, you can gauge the effectiveness of your message by asking, "Did they buy it?" Successful people are intensely focused on the results they achieve with their customers or clients. Bob Giaimo, founder of the American Cafe and Silver Diner restaurants spends tremendous energy designing menus. However brilliant his design, there is only one criterion that ultimately counts for him: do the customers like it?

Regardless of how clever you think you are or how marvelous you consider your material to be, the only real measurement for the success of a presentation is what your customers—the audience—are able to digest. Most of us, unfortunately, grew up with a model of communication that was not customer focused.

Remember when you were in school and a classmate asked a question not directly related to the discussion. Your teacher probably responded, "We don't have time to talk about that, we must get through the curriculum." Many of us grew up with an emphasis on covering the material at the expense of actual learning. As a result, we find it easier to focus on getting through the curriculum than getting through to the audience.

Also, the more you know about your subject and the harder you have worked researching it, the easier it is to get lost in the material. This is particularly true among engineers, scientists, and other technically oriented individuals. A corporate chemist dubbed this phenomenon "molecule fondling," and defines it as the tendency to focus, in exhaustive detail, on technical points that interest only the speaker.

There is another major impediment to effectively targeting your message. The fear of failure and embarrassment often leads people to focus inordinately on themselves instead of the audience. This survival-focused, narcissistic bias acts as a communication prophylactic.

Of course, your curriculum is important, but it becomes meaningful only when it is transferred to your audience. To complete this transfer successfully, approach your presentation with more than avoidance of embarrassment as your objective. Instead, set your objectives in terms of the results you want for your audience. Do this by writing out simple answers to the following questions:

- What do you want your audience to *know* as a result of your presentation?
- How would you like them to *feel*?
- What *action* do you want them to take, what do you want them to *do*?

In a recent presentation to 500 sales representatives from a pharmaceutical company, my objectives were to be sure that at the conclusion of the hour allotted they would:

- Know—the five keys to giving an unforgettable sales presentation
- Feel—energized, enthusiastic, and confident in their ability to apply the five principles
- Act—by applying the five principles to measurably improve their sales performance

To set and achieve objectives effectively, you must know something about your audience. The more you know, the easier it becomes to target your message accurately.

When you are invited to speak, seek answers to these questions.

- How many people will attend?
- What is their level of professional training and experience?
- What is the age, gender, and cultural distribution?
- What are their expectations?
- Who are the decision makers in the audience?
- Are any recent events or forthcoming deadlines impinging on their attention?
- Have they been required to attend?
- Do they have any special sensitivities, prejudices, or "hot buttons" that should be avoided or approached with caution?

Your best source for answers is usually the person who invites you to speak. Don't be shy about asking for information that you need to do a great job. In addition to those questions, you might ask, "Is there anything else you can tell me about this group?"

If possible, interview others who have addressed the same group. Another good way to get to know your audience is to arrive early and meet them before you speak. By greeting and informally interviewing members of your group, you will be able to fine-tune your presentation while building rapport in advance.

I was once scheduled to lead a seminar on memory and creative thinking for a group of auto company managers in Flint, Michigan. I arrived early and mingled with the audience. They told me that they had just discovered that 40 percent of them were about to lose their jobs as the result of plant closings. With the help of a quick mind mapping session I reorganized my presentation to focus on helping them meet the challenges of this crisis.

The positive results obtained by targeting your message are illustrated in a story Harvey Mackay tells about Toots Shor, New York's legendary restaurateur. Apparently Shor liked to conduct informal market research by pretending he was from out of town and asking strangers for advice on where to eat. One day, he got into a cab and asked the driver to suggest a fine restaurant.

The driver responded, "Toots Shor's is the place to go. I recommend it to all my passengers and they always love it. The atmosphere is great, the service is tops, and the food can't be beat."

As the driver maneuvered through traffic en route to the restaurant, he continued to sing the praises of the Shor establishment. As they drove up to the entrance, the thrilled restaurateur pulled out a roll of cash, peeled off a hundred-dollar bill, and handed it to the cabbie. He told him to keep the change.

"Gosh," exclaimed the driver, "thanks a lot, Mr. Shor."

KISS—Keep It Simple, Speaker

A great presentation is like an iceberg: the point is clear and the vast majority of the content is below the surface. Although you should always be prepared with much more material than you will actually use, it is best to make your presentation as short and simple as possible. Brevity *is* the soul of wit; simplicity is its spirit.

Condensing and simplifying your material has two major benefits. It pushes you to a deeper understanding of your own thoughts, and it makes it much more likely that your audience will stay awake.

Many presenters suffer from the illusion that they can effectively communicate a lot of detailed, complex information in an oral presentation. One reason this illusion is so prevalent is the example set by many college professors and other academics who try to prove their brilliance by making incomprehensible presentations. Perhaps this is why, in the business world, the word *academic* is frequently used as a synonym for *irrelevant*.

Detailed, complex information is best communicated in writing with a supplementary oral presentation that emphasizes the key points while allowing time for a question-and-answer session.

To be brief is almost a condition of being inspired.
—George Santayana

Unless obfuscation is your aim, you will never compromise your effectiveness by simplifying your material. As the brilliant anthropologist Margaret Mead observed: "If one cannot state a matter clearly enough so that even an intelligent twelve year old can understand it, one should remain within the cloistered walls of the university and laboratory until one gets a better grasp of one's subject matter."

Set the Stage

A few years ago, I was invited, on two days' notice, to speak at a conference for the external affairs and public relations division of one of the world's largest telecommunications companies. The purpose of the conference was to build support for a new advertising strategy, which included moving the company's entire $50 million advertising budget to a new agency. The conference slogan was, "You'll Take Us There!"

The company hired the grand ballroom at a luxury hotel and spent a fortune on mock-ups of the new ad campaign. They provided a comprehensive, beautifully produced handout and first-class refreshments. I was offered a princely sum to speak for eight and a half minutes on "Meeting the Challenge of Change."

Arriving early to get to know my audience and check out the environment, I discovered that the seating and stage arrangement was a setup for disaster. The audience of more than 400 people was to be kept in the dark, as spotlights focused on corporate honchos perched on a dias that seemed as high as Mount Olympus. The speakers were scheduled to make their presentations from behind enormous podiums. I also discovered that the podiums had control buttons allowing speakers to adjust their height.

Although management aimed to deliver a message of inclusion, empowerment, and inspiration, the audience was likely to feel alienated, distanced, and patronized.

I quickly mind mapped a new slant on my presentation, and consulted with the lighting and stage crew. I took a seat at the back of the darkened ballroom and awaited my turn to speak. After being introduced, I strode briskly up the center aisle (in the dark), leaped onto the stage, and stepped behind the podium. Like the speakers who preceded me, I projected nothing more than a talking head.

I started to talk about change and the pressure and anxiety it creates, and how anxiety can create barriers between people when they need to find a new approach to teamwork. As I said the word *barriers,* I pressed the "up" button, and as I continued to speak, the podium rose and I slowly disappeared from view. Unseen for about twenty seconds, I expounded without pause on the challenge of change and its effects on communication.

Then, talking about the importance of moving beyond barriers, I emerged from behind the podium and jumped off the stage. Standing in the spotlight, I urged the audience to recognize their power to make a difference—to create the kind of corporate culture they wanted. As I emphasized the theme of self-empowerment, the spotlights shifted to focus on the audience and they exploded with spontaneous applause.

Use your environment to empower your message. As Marshall McLuhan said, "The medium is the message." The environment in which you make your presentation sometimes communicates more strongly than your words. You probably won't need to make the dramatic alterations that were required in my presentation, but you can increase your effectiveness by creating a brain-nourishing environment for your audience.

Consider these factors when you create a brain-nourishing environment.

SPACE, AMBIANCE, AND FURNITURE

An uncomfortable, crowded room is no place for effective communication. Arrange for an ample, well-lit space and pleasing decor. A few green plants and a bouquet of fresh flowers can work wonders. Set up chairs or tables to suit your purpose. Remove excess chairs and other unnecessary objects, such as charts or audiovisual equipment left over by a previous speaker. Before you begin, put yourself in the audience's position: sit in the back row and imagine what it's like to participate in your presentation.

AUDIOVISUAL AIDS

Appropriate use of audio and visual aids dramatically improves the impact, efficiency, and memorability of meetings and presentations. Test and practice with projectors, flip charts, and videos before using them. Make certain that visuals can be clearly seen from all parts of the room. If you are using electronic equipment, be prepared for it to fail. If you must use a microphone, insist on a cordless collar clip-on; it encourages freedom of movement and allows consistent voice modulation.

Apply the KISS principle, making all your visuals simple and clear. Follow Margaret Mead's advice—if an intelligent twelve year old couldn't understand your visual, don't use it. Employ the fewest visuals needed to emphasize your key points. A slide presentation can almost always be improved by eliminating half the slides. Show pictures that are *worth* a thousand words, not pictures *of* a thousand words.

APPEARANCE

Your appearance is your most powerful visual. Despite admonitions not to "judge books by their covers," audiences will judge you by yours. Most audiences scrutinize every detail of a speaker's grooming and dress. Did you miss a spot shaving? Is your blouse the wrong size? Are your shoes unshined? Tie doesn't match? If you are not sure, at the first break, slip into a rest-room stall, have a seat, and listen to the conversations around you.

To avoid becoming the subject of negative rest-room reviews, and to be sure that your appearance doesn't distract from your message, heed this advice.

- Dress and groom yourself so that you feel comfortable and confident. When in doubt, be conservative.
- Wear clothes that fit well, in colors and fabrics that are complementary to one another and to you.
- Pay attention to detail. Shine your shoes, check your makeup, button your jacket, use a lint brush. Look your best and enjoy it.
- Be slightly better dressed than your audience. Most professional and corporate organizations are like the military. If you are with a group of majors and you wear the uniform of a corporal, they'll send you out for coffee. Dress like a colonel and they'll salute.

A note on distractions: if you set your stage appropriately, you will preempt most distractions. Nevertheless, from time to time, you may be confronted with inoperative air conditioners, exploding overhead projectors, jackhammer choruses from the street, and bomb scares. Whatever the distraction, acknowledge the problem with good humor and act with common sense. Strange as it seems, if a speaker fails to call attention to a continuing distraction, an audience tends to blame the speaker for it.

Use Mind Maps

Mind mapping makes preparing, remembering, and delivering presentations faster, easier, and much more fun. By encouraging you to think synvergently, mind mapping makes it much more likely that you will capture your audience's whole brain. The free-flowing, image-rich, colorful format helps produce imaginative and colorful presentations. And because mind mapping is a natural, brain-friendly method for generating and organizing ideas, it helps you deliver your message more confidently, authentically.

Try preparing your next presentation using a mind map. Begin by drawing a picture or symbol that represents your topic in the center of a big sheet of paper. Then print key words on connected lines. Treat this first step in preparing your content as the generation phase of the problem-solving process. Suspend judgment and go for quantity of ideas.

When you feel that you have generated enough material, shift to the evaluation mode and analyze how your ideas fit together. Create your own symbol and color codes to show relationships. Look for keys words that appear repeatedly in different branches of your map; they often suggest integrating themes. Next, redraw your mind map, organizing the material in clockwise rotation, and number your main branches. Draw a picture or symbol to represent each key point.

Besides helping you prepare your presentation faster and more creatively, mind mapping makes it easier to remember your material. Many presentations are compromised by the need to read a script or sort through file cards. You've probably heard stories about speakers who were accidentally given double copies of their scripts, and read each page twice to their audience!

The less dependent you are on notes, the more confident and authoritative you will be. Pictures, symbols, and key words are much easier to remember than sentences or outlines. To take full advantage of mind mapping as a presentation mnemonic device, apply the mind map memory method. Make your mind map, then put it aside and re-create it from memory on a blank sheet of paper. Do this until you can re-create your mind map perfectly.

Then hang your mind map on the wall or attach it to the ceiling above your bed, close your eyes, and practice picturing your key words and symbols in your mind's eye. Open your eyes and check your progress. After doing this a few times, your notes will be unforgettable.

Of course, you also should rehearse your presentation in more traditional ways. Practice your presentation until it feels natural. If possible, get feedback by using audio- or videotape. Complement your rehearsal with mental practice. Visualize success. See yourself calmly taking command of the stage. Imagine the feeling of making contact with your audience. Listen to the mellifluous sound of your voice as you deliver your message. Most important, maintain a positive "I can" attitude from the beginning, even before you have figured out what you're going to say.

If you anticipate resistance or hostility from your audience, make a devil's advocate mind map, noting every possible objection or assault you might encounter. Then, as part of your presentation, articulate the opposing points of view and address them empathically. By posing and then answering challenges skillfully you build rapport and disarm antagonists. If the presentation is particularly important, invite a few friends or colleagues to play the role of the most obnoxious audience imaginable. Every president since Kennedy has applied this rehearsal method in dealing with the press. Bill Clinton's former communications director, George Stephanopolous, helped prepare his boss for a major press conference on the Balkan crisis by asking the president during a rehearsal: "Is your policy in Bosnia designed to promote ethnic cleansing?"

Whether you like it or not, presentations are always a form of theater. The only question is, Will it be good theater or bad? Any good actor will tell you that rehearsal is a key to success.

The dream of many young actors is that the star of the show will fall ill and that they will make their name by stepping in at the last minute. For most business and professional people, however, this dream is more of a nightmare. Business people tell harrowing stories of having to write scripts at the last minute to prepare for unexpected speaking engagements and other surprises. If you find, for example, that the presenter preceding you covered half of what you had planned to say, or that the keynote speaker just canceled and you are asked to fill in, you must be able to improvise. Mind mapping makes it easier to adapt to changing circumstances.

An executive vice president of a chain of hardware stores used mind mapping to deal with last-minute changes involving an important speech to a March of Dimes conference. As honorary chairman for his metropolitan area, he was invited to be the introductory speaker at an important luncheon. A local television news anchor was scheduled to follow him as keynote speaker.

"My typewritten remarks had been sent to me a few days prior to the meeting [and] were to be read to the group," he wrote. "Arriving at the luncheon, I was told that [the anchor man] was sick and would not be able to attend. Therefore, they had no keynote speaker." Sensing their panic, he asked if they would like him to handle the keynote portion of the presentation. They agreed.

He went off into a corner for ten minutes and drew a mind map, tying in his typed remarks with personal associations relating to preventing birth defects. When it came time for his speech, he reported, "The portion that I had mind mapped was infinitely better than the prewritten remarks."

In addition to its value in preparing, memorizing, and adapting your presentations, you can use mind mapping to improve your delivery. With the aid of an overhead projector, mind map your presentation for your audience as you deliver it. You can begin by saying something like, "I am going to make a simple map of the ideas I will be presenting." If you want your audience to take notes (research shows that note taking, especially in mind map form, dramatically improves understanding and recall), add, "Please map along with me."

As images and key words are linked before their eyes, in rhythm with your voice, you create clear connections in the minds of your audience. Using mind maps in this way captures your audience's imagination. Your presentation becomes easy to follow and hard to forget.

With mind mapping, you're more creative in generating and thinking through ideas. You'll have more confidence in your delivery because you're better able to remember what you plan to say. Mind mapping also encourages you to be more spontaneous. You won't worry about departing from a script.

One caveat: build the mind map for your audience *as* you speak and do not try to present a complete mind map to a group that is unfamiliar with the process.

A vice president of a multinational computer company once ignored this warning. He was so proud of a five-year strategic planning mind map that he had created with his senior team that he had it color copied and sent to his entire organization. Accompanying the map was a brief memo: "Five-Year Plan—Implement!" For weeks, his employees tried desperately to decipher his mind map. He later realized that he would have gotten far better results with a step-by-step approach.

Make Friends with Your Fear

According to the *Book of Lists,* public speaking is the number-one fear of most people. It is greater than the fear of nuclear war, financial ruin, or getting mugged. Death ranks seventh on the list. In other words, most people would rather be resting in the casket than giving the eulogy. Why are people so afraid of public speaking? Because it reminds them of the "Ha Ha Ha, you idiot" syndrome they experienced in their early years of schooling. The potential for embarrassment and humiliation makes the fear of public speaking an immediate, pressing force in daily life, and often causes people to avoid speaking altogether. Others grit their teeth and march up to speak like condemned prisoners walking to the gallows. Armoring themselves with glazed eyes, frozen posture, and a monotone voice, they try to ignore, suppress, or deny their fear while cowering behind the podium.

The first key to transforming fear is understanding that the feeling is universal. There is nothing wrong with it. Even professional actors, including greats such as Helen Hayes, Carol Burnett, and Sir Alec Guinness regularly experience intense nervousness before performing. Once acknowledged and accepted, fear becomes a fuel for keener alertness, motivation, and enthusiasm. You can make fear your ally.

BE HERE NOW

Many people practice negative, unconscious visualization, commonly known as worry. Examine your worries. You will find that they are focused on the past ("My last presentation was a fiasco") or the future ("What if I lose my place and they all start laughing at me?"). Your life, however, is always taking place in the present. When you bring your awareness into the present moment by, for example, attending to the flow of your breathing or making eye contact with your audience, you are able to be your best.

FOCUS ON YOUR AUDIENCE

One of the synvergent secrets of a happy life is balancing self-awareness and concern with focus and care for the needs of others. The same is true for a great presentation. Nervousness can suck you into the quicksand of extreme introspection. It leads you to scrutinize and exaggerate your weaknesses, perverting consciousness of self into self-consciousness. Although healthy self-examination is useful before and after your presentation, you want to pay more attention to your audience than to yourself while you are speaking.

Great presenters know a secret about transforming fear. In most situations, *the audience is nervous.* Why do you think people hide in the back row, leaving the front seats empty? Perhaps they remember the humiliation of being called on by the teacher when they were unprepared. Whatever the reason, group situations magnify the potential for embarrassment. As the speaker, you are in a position of power and control. Take care of your audience. Help them relax and enjoy your message. Direct your attention to their needs. If you focus on fulfilling the objectives you set for them, you won't have the time or the need to indulge your anxiety.

Warm Up and Stretch Before You Speak

Fear releases powerful hormones into your bloodstream, with corresponding muscular contractions. This reaction, called the fight-or-flight response, is instinctive. Nature designed it to mobilize us to escape from, or fight with, would-be predators.

During speaking engagements, however, it's generally not good form to dash out of the room or to physically assault the audience. So most speakers just sit there, tightening up and stewing in their own stress juices as they wait their turn. Instead of basting in anxiety, find a private space and do some mind/body warm-up exercises. You will metabolically transform your stress hormones and begin to release the corresponding patterns of muscular contraction. If you already have a warm-up stretching routine that you do prior to exercise, begin with that. In addition, try some of these prepresentation warm-ups:

MAKE FUNNY FACES

Fear can lead you to take your presentation, and yourself, far too seriously. This overseriousness often manifests by freezing your face into a rigid, zombielike mask. Do what professional actors do and save face by making funny faces. Standing in front of a mirror, make the most fearful look you can muster. Experiment with a full range of exaggerated expressions. Try anger, surprise, sadness, and joy. Finish by making the stupidest faces imaginable. Let your jaw slacken as your tongue hangs out. Besides encouraging a more lighthearted attitude, these exercises mobilize your face and make you look and feel more relaxed and expressive. If you practice looking like an idiot before you present, you're less likely to look like one while you speak.

LIBERATE YOUR BREATH AND VOICE

Observe the flow of your breathing. Let your consciousness float on the rhythmic tide of inspiration and release. As you inhale, imagine the breath filling your entire body, right down to your toes. Allow a complete, extended exhalation. Complete seven cycles, allowing each breath to be deeper than the one before.

Then let the release of your breath become a sound. As you exhale, think of something amusing. Smile and whisper "Aahhhhhh. . . ." After three or four whispered ahhhhhs, let yourself sigh and yawn. Then hum your favorite tune. After humming for a minute, break into song. Sing your favorite inspirational song. Then, sing the first few lines of your presentation. These simple breathing and vocalizing exercises will prevent you from "choking up" while expanding the resonance and freedom of your voice.

SHADOWBOX

Although it is not appropriate to express the fight-or-flight response by fighting with an audience, one of the best ways to transform the accumulated energy is to act out running and fighting behaviors. Runners and racquetball players know that a good run or intense game is the quickest and most effective way to shift out of a tense, stressed state. If you can't run or pound a ball against the wall, try shadowboxing. Dance around and throw some punches. Here is a little rhyme to inspire you.

Start by pretending you're Muhammad Ali;
Float like a butterfly, sting like a bee.
Dance around, bob and weave,
Feel those jitters beginning to leave.

Throw your left and follow with a cross
The audience'll know that you're the boss
Follow the advice in this rhyme
and you will be the greatest of all time!

If you acknowledge your fear, center yourself in the present, focus on your audience and warm-up, you will be set up for success. But in dealing with stage fright, we need all the help we can get. Keep the following ideas in mind—they'll help you relax and be your best.

You tend to look much better than you feel. Although you may feel very nervous, the audience generally won't know it. Adrenaline causes you to exaggerate your perceptions, making you imagine that a grammatical error or awkward movement is a massive gaffe. The audience probably never even notices it. Relax. And remember, even if you are feeling shaky, you probably look better than you feel.

Audiences generally want you to succeed. Inexperienced speakers often imagine that audiences are composed of rejects from *The Gong Show*, desperately yearning to wreak their revenge. In reality, most audiences are supportive. They want you to succeed.

People generally attend presentations with the hope of gaining something from the time they invest. They have a stake in your success. Moreover, people tend to identify with the challenge of speaking, and usually are quite tolerant of your imperfections.

Your audience is made up of individuals. Many people are comfortable and effective speaking to one or two others, but put them in front of a group of twenty or thirty listeners and things change dramatically. Although large groups can provide a sense of anonymity, it is a mistake to imagine that you are addressing an impersonal mass.

However large your audience, it is always individual brains that receive and process your message.

The principles of effective communication are the same whether you speak to an individual or a group. Empathy, flexibility, and authenticity are the keys to successful one-to-one communication; the same is true for groups. The main difference in communicating with a group is the extent to which you project your voice and body language to reach your audience. The larger your audience, the more you must magnify your natural movements, gestures, and vocal projection.

An audience doesn't expect much. A basic truth of life is that satisfaction is a function of expectation. Expectation is usually a function of experience. If a friend is accustomed to eating at Denny's, he will be impressed if you take him to Sizzler's. If you make an effort to apply the simple tools expressed in this chapter, you will easily exceed most audience's expectations.

Enjoy yourself! Audiences mirror the inner state of a speaker. If you are bored and disinterested, the audience will feel the same. If you are enthusiastic and inspired, the audience will follow your lead. Poet W. B. Yeats summed it up: "I always think a great orator convinces us, not by force of reasoning, but because he is visibly enjoying the beliefs he wants us to accept."

Cultivate Articulate Body Language

In Japan, people greet one another with a bow. The traditional salutation in India is the *namaste,* a slight bow with hands in the prayer position. Hugs and embraces are common in the Middle East, Latin America—and Southern California. Elsewhere, the handshake reigns. What do all these gestures have in common? They are all body language messages, designed to reassure the repto-mammalian brain by conveying the message "I am friend, not foe."

Just as we reassure one another with physical language, we communicate trustworthiness or the lack thereof. People who appear shifty-eyed, twisted, or crooked are viewed with suspicion; those who are level-headed, straightforward, and upright are perceived as honest.

Your posture, gestures, expressions, and voice tone communicate far more than your words. If your body language is inconsistent with your words, the audience will believe your body. Prof. Albert Mehrabian's classic studies demonstrated that when a person's words and appearance seem inconsistent, credibility is determined 55 percent from body language, 38 percent from voice tone, and 7 percent from actual content.

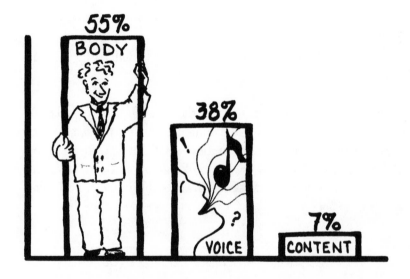

People automatically respond to the way your body language and voice quality mesh with your words. Are your posture, movement, gestures, facial expression, eye contact, voice tone, volume, and inflection in synch with your message? This "body message synchrony" is a natural product of authenticity.

Beware of the man whose stomach does not move when he laughs.
—ancient chinese proverb

Cynics in Hollywood say, "Sincerity is the key to success. Once you can fake that, you've got it made." Some presentation courses aim to teach you how to fake authority through power gestures and dominant body language. It's better to allow your true authority to emerge by cultivating body language that is natural, expressive, and authentic. This involves "unlearning" unnecessary habits that constrain self-expression. Although the elements of body language always function interdependently, we can simplify our approach to "unlearning" by considering them individually.

POSTURE AND MOVEMENT

In a study conducted at Rahway State Prison in New Jersey, a group of muggers was shown videotapes of people walking down the street, and asked to rate their "muggability." As you might expect, individuals who displayed an obvious infirmity in their movement were rated most muggable. The muggers also targeted people who moved in a stiff, slumped, awkward, or aggressive fashion. The least muggable were those with an upright carriage and a relaxed but purposeful gait.

As you walk to the front of a room to speak, the audience instinctively assesses your muggability. Standing and moving in a poised manner preempts resistance and improves your stage presence dramatically.

The most challenging aspect of an actor's training is not memorizing complex soliloquies or learning strange accents; a would-be thespian's greatest challenge is learning to stand and move in an expansive, natural, unaffected way. You can cultivate these qualities by developing a basic posture or stance for presenting.

Begin by standing with your feet about shoulder-width apart, sensing the feeling of your feet firmly on the floor. Keep your knees free without bending them. Allow your shoulders to release as your arms rest easily at your sides. Let your neck be free so that your head can float at the top of your lengthening spine. Keep your eyes alert and alive.

Practice this basic stance in front of a mirror. How long can you stand without fidgeting or stiffening? Practice the stance in the course of everyday conversation. Are you able to just *be* with others without making unnecessary gestures or movements? A reliable basic stance conveys openness and dignity, and becomes a point of departure for graceful, confident movement.

Your movements have tremendous power to sabotage or reinforce your message. Unconscious rocking and swaying movements might be fine if you are speaking about drunkenness or the perils of ocean travel. Otherwise, they will distract or even nauseate your listeners.

If your movements are in synch with the flow of communication, they add depth and resonance. The human brain is designed to follow movement. For example, if you were to talk about the difference between left and right brain, you might naturally move from the left to the right side of the stage.

To discover and unlearn your unnecessary, unconscious movements, watch yourself on video and seek feedback from a friend. While learning to let go of distracting movements, avoid the trap of standing frozen in place. If you are not confident in your movement, invest more time exploring the basic stance. With practice you will discover this synvergent insight: movement is the secret of stillness, and stillness the secret of movement. In the words of the legendary theater director Peter Brook: "Standing still has to be the ultimate achievement of a body that can move. . . ."

GESTURES

Over twenty years ago, some friends and I spent a summer traveling through Italy. We arrived in Rome with a list of three recommended *pensione,* inexpensive bed-and-breakfast hotels. The first place on our list, Pensione Rosa, had no vacancies. The second, Pensione Alberto, was also full. We asked the owner if he could tell us if we were likely to find room at Pensione Anna, the last place on our list.

Alberto responded by repeating the name Pensione Anna as he drew his sleeve, all the way from his shoulder to his fingertips, across his nose. He completed this gesture of unqualified disgust by casting a large quantity of imaginary nasal discharge violently to the floor. His gesture was so powerful that more than two decades later if a friend mentions traveling to Rome, I'm quick to warn, "Don't stay at Pensione Anna!"

Gestures have tremendous impact on your effectiveness as a communicator. There are two keys to making that impact positive. The first is to avoid unnecessary gestures. Change rattling, pen fondling, face scratching, and genital guarding are among the most common nervous gestures that create unintended results. Observe yourself in a mirror or on video, and pare superfluous gestures from your presentation. If you aren't sure what to do with your hands, just allow them to rest at your sides.

The second key is to discover your natural gestural language and exaggerate it. Although you do not have to go as far as Alberto, you can increase your impact by telling your story with your hands. Let your natural gestural language emerge and expand. Just as you need to increase the projection of your voice to reach a large group, you must project your gestures.

Shyness leads many people to suppress their natural gestural expression. With appropriate feedback, however, this self-limitation can be overcome. An executive of a Swedish shipping company provides a delightful example of this point. In a presentation meant to describe his company's most impressive vessel, he held his hands in front of his chest no more than a few inches apart. As he watched himself on video, he realized that this was not an accurate gestural representation of his company's flagship. His smile suggested that he understood the need to move beyond his self-imposed constraint.

In the next "take," he doubled the size of his gesture. But the video clearly demonstrated that his gestural frame was still too small for the picture he intended to convey. Mustering his courage for a final take, he flung his arms to full horizontal extension while booming out the words, "we have *really* big tanker." Later, when he watched the tape, he was amazed to discover that the gesture, which had felt grossly exaggerated to him, actually looked natural and appropriately expressive.

You can awaken your natural expression by watching yourself on video. Study how your exaggerated gestures complement your message. Other useful exercises include miming your presentation, experimenting with gestures in everyday conversation, and playing charades.

EYE CONTACT

When Muhammad Ali fought Joe Frazier in the Thrilla in Manilla, he stared intensely into Frazier's eyes while the referee recited the rules. At the end of *Casablanca,* Ingrid Bergman and Humphrey Bogart gaze deeply into each other's eyes, communicating volumes of heart-wrenching emotion.

Eyes express the full range of human experience, from threat and terror to profound intimacy and passion. Of course, in most presentations you are not looking to stare down or romance your audience. Your aim is to make contact so you can keep their interest and communicate your message. Eye contact enables you to read your audience and monitor your effectiveness. Is your audience bored? Are they confused? Enraptured? Tired? The answer is in front of your eyes.

Practice seeing with alert, receptive "listening" eyes. When you engage people's eyes in an open and fully present manner, you establish trust, draw interest, and access channels of influence. Although relatively easy in one-to-one communication, many speakers find it difficult to make eye contact with people in groups. The difficulty usually stems from viewing the audience as an impersonal mass. However large your audience, speak to them as individuals.

If you are uncomfortable making eye contact with an audience, try this exercise. While you're standing on stage, pick out the friendliest-looking people sitting to your right, your left, and straight in front. Use them as anchors for eye contact. Engage their eyes for four or five seconds at a time. By focusing on representatives from each part of the room, you give the whole audience a greater sense of your involvement and interest in them. As you become comfortable with your anchors, expand your gaze to "meet" other members of the audience.

When you master this, try a more challenging exercise. Seek out the *unfriendliest*-looking people from each part of the room, and draw them out by engaging their eyes in a confident and friendly manner. I once attempted this while giving an after-dinner speech to a group of investment bankers. The group was just finishing an elaborate meal that had begun with cocktails and proceeded through several wine-accompanied courses. As they sniffed their cognac and settled back in their chairs, I rose to deliver my remarks.

Among the many bored, tired, and downright hostile candidates for anchors, I chose three granite-faced bankers who seemed committed to acting as though there were no speaker. Launching into the presentation, I sought them out with my eyes, looking beyond their apparent disinterest. Halfway through the speech, two of the three shifted their positions. Their postures opened and their eyes said they were with me. The third fellow remained slumped over, arms tightly folded, expressionless.

As I began my closing, I could see from the nods and thoughtful looks that the audience, with the exception of my third anchor, was getting the message. I made one last attempt to draw him out with my eyes, to no avail. Finally, I spoke my last sentence—just as he passed out and collapsed on the floor!

I can't guarantee 100 percent success—or that you'll win over two out of three hostile listeners and knock the third one cold. But you will find that natural, lively eye contact is a great way to enliven your communication.

VOICE

To appreciate the effect that your voice has on your communication, try a little experiment. Pick any sentence or phrase and alter its meaning by changing your tone, inflection, and volume. For example, try to make the words "Yes, I am sure you are right" mean "No, I am sure you are wrong."

In addition to inverting the meaning of words, your voice can express an amazing range of complexities and nuances of meaning. According to Professor Mehrabian, your vocal usage accounts for approximately 38 percent of your credibility when your audience sees you, and up to 84 percent when they don't (over the telephone or on radio, for example).

What are the secrets of a great voice?

EXPRESSIVE VARIATION

Do you know why you are able to fall asleep despite the rumblings of your air conditioner or the sounds of traffic passing outside the window? Your brain contains a marvelous system called the reticular activating mechanism. It tunes out repetitive noise. The same mechanism wakes you in response to a sound that stands out from a monotonous background, such as your alarm ringing.

Unfortunately for boring speakers, the reticular activating mechanism also helps an audience sleep through presentations delivered in a monotone voice. By varying your tone, inflection, and volume in co-ordination with your content, you send a stream of wake-up calls to your audience's brains, dramatically increasing the impact and memorability of your presentation.

THE PAUSE

Um, ah, the pause is, you know, uh, like, a really important part of, ah, using the, ah, voice. The average speaker is afraid to pause. As a result, most people either talk too fast or use filler noises such as "um," "ah," "you know," and "like."

In the *Tao Te Ching*, Lao Tzu offers these synvergent reflections:

> *Thirty spokes are made one by holes in a hub,*
> *By vacancies joining them for a wheel's use;*
> *The use of clay in molding pitchers*
> *comes from the hollow of its absence;*
> *Doors, windows in a house,*
> *Are used for their emptiness;*
> *Thus we are helped by what is not,*
> *to use what is.*

The pause is the hub, the hollow, that brings your words to life. Pausing gives you time to breathe, to center yourself, to think. It gives your audience the opportunity to absorb and reflect upon your message. Pausing conveys confidence as it captivates your audience's attention.

Develop your "pauseability" by listening to yourself on tape. Experiment with extending your pauses. Explore appropriate timing. Notice your frequency of filler words, and strive to eliminate them. Instead of um-ing and ah-ing, pause.

POSTURE AND BREATHING

Your voice rides on your breath. Free breathing liberates your voice, and a balanced, expansive upright posture frees your breathing. As you develop your basic stance and ease of movement, your breathing and voice will improve.

Despite a grueling speaking schedule and occasional bouts with hay fever and flu, I have never lost my voice. I apply a method that gives me access to the natural, expressive, and authentic use of my voice and body language. This same method is also an effective means for developing self-knowledge, changing habits, and transforming fear. It is the Alexander technique referred to in the discussion of psychophysical fitness in the first chapter. The technique is taught at the world's premiere theater and music schools, such as the Julliard School and the Royal Academies of Drama and Music. It's a trade secret of many of the world's great performing artists, including Paul Newman, Joanne Woodward, Sting, John Cleese, Mary Steenburgen, Sir George Solti, Paul McCartney, John Houseman, Jennifer Jason-Leigh, Hal Holbrook, and Sir Ian McKellen. Lessons in the Alexander technique will improve your poise, breathing, voice, and overall presentation power.

The PROPAR Approach: Putting It All Together

No matter how well prepared and poised a speaker is, a presentation is effective only if the audience *remembers* what the speaker wants them to remember.

A common pitfall in communication is confusing understanding with remembering. Your audience may nod in apparent understanding, but that does not ensure that they will remember. Of course, remembering without understanding would not be very useful either.

Effective communication requires the integration of understanding and recall. The PROPAR approach holds the secret of that integration. PROPAR is an acronym for the five principles that organize recall during a presentation: primacy, repetition, outstandingness, personal association, and recency.

Consider the average presentation. What parts of it are you most likely to remember? Most people would say the beginning and the end, and they're right. People tend to remember the first thing that happens in a series, and the last. In fact, it often happens that people are awake for the first few minutes of a presentation, then they fall asleep during the middle, and wake up just at the end!

The tendency to remember first impressions is known as the primacy effect. The tendency to remember the last thing is called the recency effect.

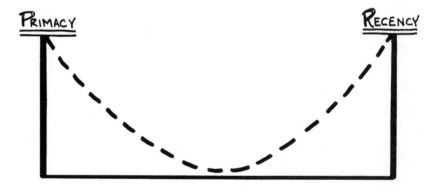

How can you take advantage of the primacy and recency effect and raise your audience out of the trough in the middle?

It's possible for a speaker to raise the audience out of the trough in the middle (see diagram). Besides remembering the first and last elements in a series, we recall anything that is repeated, outstanding, or unusual, and anything that has a special personal association for us. Taken together, these five principles of recall form a simple and powerful strategy for great presentations. Let's look at the applications of each one.

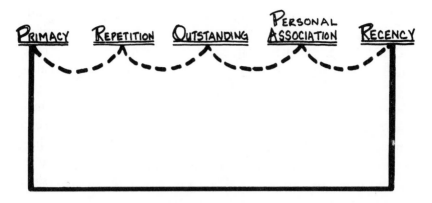

The PROPAR approach holds the secret of integrating understanding and recall.

THE PRIMACY EFFECT

If your boss comes into the office on a Monday morning and says, "We are going on a trip," the first question likely to come to your mind would be, "Where are we going?" Once the destination is known, your next question might be, "Why are we going there?" You'd probably follow that with, "How are we going to get there?"

A presentation is a journey of communication. An audience wants to know where you plan to take them, why they should go with you, and how you are going to get them there. So, in the first few minutes of your presentation:

Make contact with your audience. If your boss is a skilled communicator, he will take time to establish personal contact before announcing the trip. A simple, sincere, "Good morning, how are you?" accompanied by natural eye contact, sets the stage for cooperative action. It is the same when you are presenting to a group. Embrace your audience with your words and your eyes.

In 1980, Tony Buzan and I led a three-day seminar for 500 children in Soweto, South Africa. On the first morning, I walked on stage and said, "Good morning." The children, who were used to being taught by rote, responded with a lifeless, "Good morning, sir." So I said, "No, you didn't understand me, I really mean it. GOOOOD MORN-

ING!" A constellation of smiles appeared before me as 500 giggling children, their minds and hearts now open to learning, howled, "GOOOOOOOOOOOOOOOOD MORNING!"

Communicate your key points. Where are we going? In the words of the proverbial Southern preacher, "Tell 'em what yer gonna tell 'em, hallelujah!"

Frame your key points in a context of benefits for the audience. Why are we going? As you clearly relate your message to the audience's concerns, you capture and keep their attention.

Give an overview. How are we going to get there? By sharing the structure of your presentation, you mentally set the audience to remember your message. When you show them the path you'll travel, they will be much more willing to accompany you.

BODY LANGUAGE AND THE POWER OF PRIMACY

Harvard psychologist Nalini Ambady showed subjects *ten-second* long videotapes of professors lecturing. The subjects were asked to rate the effectiveness of each teacher after the brief viewing. The results were astonishing—the subject's ratings, based on ten-second exposure, correlated almost exactly with the ratings obtained from students after a full term of lectures. Further research demonstrated that subjects offered accurate evaluations after viewing video segments only *two seconds* in length. Ambady attributes this remarkable ability to read and instantly interpret body language to "evolutionary adaptation, the need to figure out who friends and foes were."

REPETITION

A great myth about communication is the belief that if you say something and your audience seems to understand it, they will remember it. If you want your audience to remember your message, you must repeat, you must repeat, you must repeat it. Tell your audience what you are going to tell them. Then tell them. And then tell them what you told them. Many of the finest speakers pause and review their key points as they make them.

Of course, intelligent use of repetition requires avoiding monotony. Use visuals and other creative means to reinforce your points. A creative and effective approach is to find a phrase that summarizes your message and rhythmically repeat the words in the manner of Dr. Martin Luther King ("I have a dream") or Muhammad Ali ("I am the greatest").

Be sure that you repeat *all* your key points. I once shared the stage with a speaker who was trying to generate support for a new educational program. In his enthusiasm for this project he repeated the phrase "It can be done!" at least fifty times in twenty minutes. His passion and commitment were unquestionable and the audience was clearly energized. Later, I asked someone what the speech was all about. He replied, "I'm not sure, but whatever it is, we can do it!"

OUTSTANDINGNESS

Left-brain imbalance and fear of embarassment ensure that most speakers take no chances with creativity. This is why most presentations are utterly forgettable. If you want your audience to remember your message—if you want your presentation to be great—you must make it outstanding or unusual.

Use humor, MAPS, visuals, drama, body language, and voice tone to emphasize your key points. Many people, no matter how frightening public speaking is for them have learned to pride themselves on making creative presentations. At the pension fund referred to earlier, for example, outstanding presentations have become part of the culture. This group's director of venture investments specializes in finding undervalued assets for his clients. Through dedicated practice he has transformed himself from a presentation-phobic into a masterful communicator. In a recent presentation he was part of a team that aimed to win control of a $7 billion savings plan from an outside firm. His task was to close the sale by convincing the board that the savings plan was an undervalued asset that would be better managed under his group's stewardship. He employed this strategy: after greeting the board members and giving them a brief overview, he tossed a handful of nickels, dimes, and quarters on the boardroom table, right in front of his boss's boss's boss. He asked, "How much is the change on the table worth?"

The board members counted up the coins. They added up to $1.50.

He suggested that the group examine the coins more carefully. They saw that one of the quarters was silver and probably worth five or six times its face value. He then urged them to inspect the quarter more carefully. One of the members noticed a small *s* on one side, checked the date, and remarked that it was a rare coin worth at least a hundred times its face value. The director collected the change and put it back in his pocket. After an extended pause he said, "This quarter (borrowed for the occasion) is just like our savings plan, an undervalued asset just sitting in our pocket. Let me show you how we can take better advantage of it." He then took them through the numbers and made a logical, compelling case. He captured the audience's whole brain and control of the $7 billion.

PERSONAL ASSOCIATION

You are chatting with a friend at a party when suddenly you hear your name being spoken across the room. Until that moment, you heard only a general din. But now your attention is captured. This is the power of personal association.

People hear and remember things that are relevant or meaningful to them. They tune out and forget things they don't care about. Having targeted your message to be relevant to your audience, you must now deliver it in a manner that maximizes their involvement.

The venture investment manager's presentation was outstanding, but the other secret of its success was his skill in getting his audience involved. By throwing coins on the table and asking the right questions, he transformed his audience from distant judges to coexplorers of his work.

How can you maximize audience involvement? The simplest way is to ask questions, both real and rhetorical. Asking an audience a rhetorical question dramatically raises their attention and recall levels. If I ask you about something you are interested in, what does it lead you to do? Think, participate, connect, and form personal associations.

In addition to asking questions, take every opportunity to get your audience involved. Try beginning a presentation by inviting the audience to try a task, test, or challenge related to the message. This instantly brings them fully into the present moment and into the role of cocreator.

The most effective presenters create a context where, through the use of exercises and questions, *the audience members discover the message for themselves.*

The word *education* comes from the root *educere*, which means "to draw forth" or "to lead out." However, many of us were raised in an environment where *educere* might have meant, "to stuff in." As a presenter and leader you are responsible for guiding the process of drawing forth, not stuffing in.

THE RECENCY EFFECT

As your presentation draws to a close, you have one last opportunity to achieve your objectives—to make certain that the audience knows, feels, and does what you want. Now you must "close the sale."

Repeat your key points (review your overview) and issue a call to action. Even better, maximize personal association by asking your audience to review the main points and to explain how they will apply what they have learned. If appropriate, ask participants to make a specific commitment to application.

The recency effect applies not only to content but also to emotion. Great presenters finish strong, building energy to a positive climax. End on a high note. Many speakers sabotage their recency effect by going on too long. Discipline yourself to finish on time, or a bit early. Like a great performer, leave them wanting more.

INTEGRATE STYLE AND SUBSTANCE

Lacking organization and clear objectives, divergent thinkers are prone to ramble. Although they love to entertain they can fall into the trap of telling jokes and stories that are amusing but *have nothing to do with the message.* On the other hand, convergent thinkers are frequently biased toward content, oblivious to the power of body language, visuals, metaphors, and other means for capturing the audience's imagination. The best presenters synergetically integrate convergent and divergent thinking. They are disciplined, organized, focused on achieving specific objectives, and they understand that **there is no business without show business.**

The Power of PROPAR

The PROPAR principles can be employed for more than just the design and delivery of a presentation. You can, for example, use them to craft a communications strategy to change an organizational culture or market a new product. To understand the full power of PROPAR, consider the strategies employed by the high-stakes communication of advertising. What happens when you are watching television and a commercial comes on? The colors on your screen get brighter and the volume gets louder, a *primacy* strategy designed to prevent you from muting or channel surfing.

Probably you have noticed a tendency of advertisers to repeat their product names incessantly. Why? Market research shows overwhelmingly that many people buy purely on name recognition.

On Route 95, outside Wilmington, Delaware, there is a huge billboard with just two words on it: "BUD LIGHT." The billboard has no pictures of ecstatic models or messages extolling the product's virtues. Just those two words. People on their way to work drive past it day after day. Anheuser-Busch knows that simple *repetition* of the name of its product will result in greater consumption.

Madison Avenue firms wage a continual war to find new ways to implant their clients' products in your brain. From Michael Jordan playing basketball with Bugs Bunny to the notorious Joe Camel, they capture your attention and your business by making their message *outstanding*.

Many advertisers also depend on another surefire method of making their message outstanding: sex. Seductive models, both male and female, hawk everything from beer, coffee, and cigarettes to health clubs, deodorant, and toothpaste. Advertisers rely on creating the following conversation in their audience's repto-mammalian minds: "Me see sex, me see product . . . me want sex, me buy product."

Some of the most sophisticated commercials emphasize *personal association.* Companies like McDonald's and AT&T specialize in creating heartwarming, deeply human scenarios that reach out and touch their audience's wallets. And all major companies engage in targeted marketing, tailoring their message to varying demographic profiles.

And how do commercials end? Usually with one last repetition of the name or phone number, or with a close-up of a celebrity's head centimeters away from the product. Sometimes they conclude with a call to action—"pick up your phone and call now"—accompanied by an attractive model dialing the number, just in case any viewers forget how to make a phone call.

Why do advertisers spend billions using PROPAR principles to create commercials that are often moronic and insulting? Because they are effective. PROPAR works, whether we like it or not. It can be used for good or evil. Gandhi, Hitler, Martin Luther King, Joseph McCarthy, Winston Churchill, Joseph Stalin, John F. Kennedy, and Ronald Reagan all intuitively applied the PROPAR approach.

One caveat: use PROPAR for good and to protect yourself from being manipulated by the banal. In our media-intensive age, there is a constant battle for your mind waged by advertisers, politicians, and social and religious groups. Use your understanding of these principles to keep your mind free and flexible as you develop your gifts as a presenter and leader.

If humanity is to pass safely through its present crisis on earth,
it will be because a majority of individuals are
now doing their own thinking.
—*Buckminster Fuller*

Conclusion
After Enlightenment, More Laundry

This chapter is designed to provide you with a positive "recency effect."

Before we review the main points and create an action plan for applying the lessons of *Thinking for a Change*, let's consider some additional applications of the PROPAR principles introduced in the previous chapter.

Beyond their value in guiding communication strategies in the workplace, you can use the PROPAR principles to improve the quality of your life in many other ways. Consider, for example, the role of primacy and recency in planning your day. As you wake up each morning, your mind moves through what psychologists call a hypnopompic state. This is the mental halfway house between sleep and wakefulness. It's a condition of extraordinary receptiveness, similar to the state induced by a hypnotist preparing to make a posthypnotic suggestion. Yet many people begin their day with a shocking buzzer alarm or a radio station that's playing an annoying jingle or a Barry Manilow song that haunts them for the rest of the day. Or perhaps you wake up to the news: a toxic spill has contaminated the local water supply . . . your company is laying off 10,000 people . . . the weather is lousy . . . your favorite team lost again . . . and now a word from our sponsor. . . ."

Instead of all that, plan for a positive primacy. Buy a combination tape-player alarm and wake up to inspiring music. When facing a challenging day, I set my alarm to play "Chariots of Fire" or Beethoven's Ninth. You choose your own inspiration.

Primacy and recency determine the rhythm of your day. This is why brain breaks are so important. Breaks are particularly crucial in maximizing the productivity of meetings. By taking regular breaks, every forty to ninety minutes, you create more primacy and recency, raising energy levels while making information more memorable.

One of the critical daily "primacies" occurs upon your return home from work. Many relationships suffer from the cumulative effects of daily negative primacy. Without conscious planning, it is all too easy to go from stress at work to stress at home. Develop a strategy that allows you and your partner to decompress and make contact before jumping into the daily challenges of living together. Bring special attention to the quality of the greetings and goodbyes you offer your loved ones. Positive primacies and recencies—a loving hug when you say goodbye to your kids in the morning or an extended moment of real eye contact with your partner upon returning from work—set the emotional tone of daily family life.

Just as waking up is the primacy of your day, going to bed provides your recency. Again, consciousness is the key. Complete your day with a positive stimulus. Listen to music, look at the stars, write in a journal, meditate, make love.

Use primacy and recency as instruments to orchestrate the rhythms of your life. In the earliest human societies, nature determined life's rhythms. People rose at sunrise and retired at sunset. They had an exquisite sensitivity to changing seasons and the movement of the heavens. As civilization progressed, religion became the primary regulator of daily experience. The wisdom of primacy and recency is manifest in the teachings of all major religions. Every spiritual tradition emphasizes prayer in the transitional times of the day: upon waking, before meals, and prior to sleeping.

In today's world, even if you love nature and consider yourself religious, the dominant influence of modern culture is the marketplace as expressed through the media. If you don't assert your priorities and nurture your consciousness, someone else will set your agenda.

The good news is that if you choose to dance to your own rhythm, you have more freedom, options, and possibilities than any previous generation. The ideas and techniques introduced in *Thinking for a Change* are designed to help you take full advantage of your abundant

options. The unifying theme of the book is the need for a way of thinking to meet the challenges of change.

And the key to this thinking is synergetically integrating convergent
and divergent perspectives to thrive on paradox. The ability to enjoy
and appreciate "oppositional truths" flows from a willingness to move
beyond habitual brain grooves, exploring new pathways through your
unlimited associational network. This approach begins with an awareness of the accelerating pace of change and the inadequacy of our fear-
based, hierarchically bound, repto-mammalian responses. It is
predicated on the courage to face our inconsistencies, in the context
of a commitment to growth and lifelong learning. This commitment
thrives on conscious optimism, especially in times of adversity.

Awareness and commitment set the stage for the cultivation of a balanced brain. You can synergize your hemispheres in many ways: by taking brain breaks, creating a brain-nourishing environment, cultivating
psychophysical ambidexterity, pursuing your ideal hobby, keeping a
journal, recording your dreams, meditating, transcending sexual stereotypes, and cultivating a win/win, both/and attitude.

Mind mapping unleashes your vast, multidimensional associative
capacity by guiding you to generate freely and organize effectively. It
strengthens your synvergent abilities—honing your focus on precise
key words while simultaneously encouraging the discovery of the maximum degree of freedom for each of your associations. As you develop
your skill at balancing logic and imagination—seeing the whole picture
by mapping a combination of the big picture and the details—you set
your planning, communication, memory, and creative problem-
solving talents into motion.

Your natural genius is further liberated as you recognize that your
brain is designed, through millions of years of evolution, to be the
most profoundly powerful solution-finding apparatus in the known
universe.

By applying your birthright of consciousness to question and expand
your mental sets, you harmonize the rhythms of more focused states—
preparation (combining probing questions with research and commitment), evaluation (playing angel, devil, and judge), and implementation
(making a clear plan while preparing to improvise) with the more dif-

fuse modes of generation (shaking up your mind with quantity, humor, and no evaluation) and incubation (pause).

Your creativity becomes reality as you rally others to your vision through synvergent communication and great presentations. Effective leaders and managers know that success springs from communication and that the art of listening is its source. To listen deeply, you use your eyes and your heart in harmony with your ears and your reason, influencing others through your openness to them. As you gracefully balance the dual truths of individual uniqueness and essential commonality, your empathy, compassion, and impact expand.

As a presenter and leader, you reach your audience's whole brain by integrating thorough research and attention to detail with empathy, *educere,* timing, and humor. Targeting clear objectives, questing for authenticity, setting the stage, making friends with fear, mastering body language, and applying the rhythms of PROPAR are more than merely presentation techniques. They offer a guide for living.

My wish is that you will apply the insights and methods of *Thinking for a Change* to deepen your personal fulfillment and professional effectiveness. To get the most from your reading, I recommend that you take a large sheet of paper and make a mind map of everything you have learned. Do this without looking back at the book.

Begin by sketching a picture or symbol in the center of the paper. This represents your interpretation of the essence of *Thinking for a Change.* Then free-associate, printing single key words on lines and adding colors, pictures, and symbols. As you re-create the contents, you strengthen new associations, enhancing your ability to recall and apply what you learned. After generating a comprehensive mind map, use your favorite color to highlight the elements that are most important to you.

Use the mind mapping process to make new connections between the key points of the book and your own experience. Then translate your most valuable learnings into goals and make an action plan to realize them.

One of the best ways to deepen your understanding and ability to apply your learning is to share it with someone else. Try preparing a presentation on the integration of leadership and management or the art of listening. Introduce a friend to mind mapping or creative problem solving as expressions of synvergent thinking.

Synvergent thinking is a simple and complex idea. I have aimed to make it as simple as possible, but as Einstein said, "Things should be made as simple as possible, not simpler." The light that illuminates the words you are reading, for example, can be simply understood as composed of particles. Yet, we also know that light is a wave. To the best of our knowledge, both are true. (In a delightful display of synvergent neologismization, some physicists have begun to refer to light as composed of "wavicles.") Physicists have declared that the existence of time cannot be proved and yet your boss probably won't accept that as an excuse for lateness. Our universe appears to unfold in a predictable, orderly way according to immutable laws, and yet, at the microcosmic level, we know that the dance of atomic particles is a random, unpredictable phenomenon.

These great truths of physics reflect the paradoxes of life.

Synvergent thinking offers you an approach that may bring you closer to your own experience of great truths. When we realize one or more of these truths through direct experience we call it enlightenment.

Enlightenment—not gradual, not sudden.
—Zen koan

And although these moments can change our lives we all tend to forget the lessons they offer. There's more work to do, people to see, places to go. More to unlearn. More laundry.

Perhaps, for example, you've had an experience that made you directly aware of the connectedness of all life or the eternal nature of the present moment. And yet, day to day, you experience your separateness and the feeling that there just isn't enough time. T. S. Eliot understood the paradox of enlightenment when he wrote, "At the end of all our journeying we shall return to the place from which we started and know it for the first time."

Sharpen your mind and enlighten your journey by thinking synvergently. Consider that you are responsible for your own experience, you control your own destiny, and that everything happens only by grace.

That life's greatest moments, whether at the ballfield, the boardroom, or the bedroom are characterized by a quality of effortlessness and flow and that great effort is often required to become susceptible to such grace (that is why humility is the soul of confidence). As you strive for success with total commitment to achieving your goals, bear in mind that fulfillment beckons you to see your goals as milestones on a continuous, joyful journey.

Life is tough and precarious. It is overflowing with abundant blessings and joy. So, look out for yourself and establish clear boundaries, remembering that happiness is greatest when you experience boundless love for others and for the divine.

We are living simultaneously in the worlds of spirit and matter.

We are challenged to be street smart with an open heart.

So, as the Sufis say, "Praise Allah and tether your camel."

Sufi master Kahlil Gibran wrote: "Beauty is eternity gazing at itself in a mirror. But you are eternity and you are the mirror."

Use the insights and skills of *Thinking for a Change* to polish that mirror.

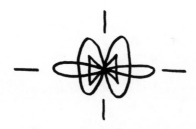

Bibliography and Reading List

In *The Power of Myth,* Bill Moyers asks Joseph Campbell how ordinary people— "those who are not poets or artists or who have not had a transcendent ecstasy"— can develop an understanding of deeper truths. Campbell offers a surprising answer: "Sit in a room and read—and read and read. And read the right books by the right people."

Here is my list of some of the right books.

Agor, Weston. *The Logic of Intuitive Decision Making.* Texas: Greenwood Press, 1986. Agor makes a strong case for the use of intuition in managing complexity.

Alexander, F. M. *The Use of Self.* New York: Dutton, 1932. Reprinted by Centerline Press, CA. 1986. The author's fascinating account of his discovery of the Alexander technique.

Bandler, Richard, and John Grinder. *Frogs into Princes: Neuro Linguistic Programming.* Utah: Real People Press, 1979. A valuable introductory work on the subject of neurolinguistic programming, a discipline that explores the fine points of nonverbal communication as well as different strategies of listening and learning.

Bennett, John Godolphin. *A Spiritual Psychology.* Revised edition. Gloucestershire, England: Coombe Springs Press, 1974. Mathematician, linguist, and visionary, Bennett devoted his extraordinary intelligence to a lifelong quest for truth.

———. *Transformation.* Gloucestershire, England: Coombe Springs Press, 1978. A manual for self-realization.

Bennis, Warren. *On Becoming a Leader.* New York: Addison-Wesley Publishing Co. Inc., 1989. Insights gained from in-depth interviews with twenty-eight leaders including James Burke, John Sculley, Betty Freidan, and Norman Lear.

Benson, Herbert. *The Relaxation Response.* London: Collins, 1976. The result of Benson's distillation of a potpourri of relaxation techniques into one simple, practical method, which can be learned from the book.

Blanchard, Kenneth, and Spencer Johnson. *The One-Minute Manager.* New York: Berkley Books, 1983. An *Elements of Style* for the art of feedback.

Block, Peter. *The Empowered Manager: Positive Political Skills at Work.* San Francisco: Jossey-Bass Inc., 1987. Strategies for understanding and overcoming the bureaucratic mind-set.

Briggs, John. *Fire in the Crucible.* Los Angeles: Jeremy P. Tarcher, Inc., 1990. An aesthetician's first-class research into the nuances of genius.

Brown, Mark. *The Dinosaur Strain: The Survivor's Guide to Personal and Business Success.* UK: Element Books, 1988. Brown is a pioneer in helping individuals and organizations develop style-flex.

Buzan, Tony, and Raymond Keene. *Buzan's Book of Genius (And How You Can Become One).* London: Stanley Paul, 1994. A systematic examination of the nature of genius with practical exercises for developing intelligences.

Buzan, Tony, and Barry Buzan. *The Mind Map Book: Radiant Thinking.* London: BBC Books, 1993. The bible of mind mapping.

Buzan, Tony. *Speed Reading.* Revised and updated. London: David & Charles, 1989. Includes the Buzan Organic Study Method and an effective approach to group learning called Commando Study.

———. *Use Both Sides of Your Brain,* 3rd ed. New York: Penguin, 1989. Buzan's classic work originally published in 1971, established him as the father of "whole-brain" education. An invaluable guide for anyone interested in learning how to learn and communicate.

———. *Use Your Memory.* Revised and updated. London: BBC Books, 1989. The best of the how-to memory books. Buzan deals with the subject comprehensively; his techniques are easy to learn and immediately applicable.

Campbell, Joseph. *The Power of Myth.* New York: Doubleday, 1988.

Celente, Gerald. *Trend Tracking.* New York: John Wiley & Sons, 1990. Create your own crystal ball.

Chopra, Deepak. *Quantum Healing: Exploring the Frontiers of Mind/Body Medicine.* New York: Bantam Books, 1989. Chopra emphasizes that "to change the printout of the body, we must alter the software of the mind."

Covey, Stephen R. *Principled-Centered Leadership.* New York: Summit Books, 1990. For seekers of a "changeless core."

———. *The 7 Habits of Highly Effective People.* New York: Simon & Schuster, Inc., 1989. Systematized common sense.

de Bono, Edward. *Six Thinking Hats.* Boston: Little, Brown & Co., 1985. My favorite de Bono book. Simple, immediately applicable tools to improve individual and team thinking.

———. *de Bono's Thinking Course.* New York: Facts on File Publications, 1982. De Bono's thinking skills are as essential as learning to read and write.

Bugental, James (ed). *The Challenge of Humanistic Psychology.* New York: McGraw-Hill, 1967. Includes a brilliant article on creativity by Arthur Koestler.

Decker, Bert. *You've Got to Be Believed to Be Heard.* New York: St. Martin's Press, 1991. Decker bases his approach to presentation and communication on the assumption that people "buy on emotion and justify with fact." Well written with many entertaining, personal examples.

Diamond, John. *Behavioral Kinesiology: The New Science for Positive Health Through Muscle Testing.* New York: Harper & Row, 1979. Diamond is a pioneer in the study of the subtle but powerful effects of environmental factors, such as lighting and music, on our mental and emotional well-being.

Dobson, Terry, and Victor Miller. *Attactics: Giving in to Get Your Way.* New York: Delacorte Press, 1978. This book demonstrates a variety of creative strategies for dealing with conflict in everyday life. Particularly valuable for the leader interested in learning how to handle difficult people.

Edwards, Betty. *Drawing on the Right Side of the Brain.* Los Angeles: Jeremy P. Tarcher, 1979. Betty Edwards's book has become a classic in the field of whole-brain education. In addition to actually learning how to draw, the careful reader will gain valuable insights into the role of imagery in thinking and creating.

Evans, Roger, and Peter Russell. *The Creative Manager.* London: Unwin, 1989.

Ferguson, Marilyn (ed). *The Brain-Mind Bulletin.* Los Angeles: Interface Press. This bulletin offers well-written abstracts on the latest advances in brain studies. I particularly recommend the reprints on left- and right-brain research.

Feynman, Richard P. *"Surely You're Joking, Mr. Feynman!"* New York: W. W. Norton & Company, 1985. A vivifying glimpse at the inner workings of one of the great minds of the twentieth century.

Fincher, Jack. *Lefties: The Origin and Consequences of Being Left-Handed.* New York: Putnam, 1977. An amusing and well-researched overview of the relationship between hand and brain.

Fisher, Roger, and William Ury. *Getting to Yes.* Boston: Houghton Mifflin Company, 1981. The classic on win-win negotiation.

Frankl, Viktor. *Man's Search for Meaning.* 3rd ed. New York: Simon & Schuster, Inc., 1984. The most inspiring book I have ever read.

Fulghum, Robert. *All I Ever Needed to Know I Learned in Kindergarten.* New York: Villard Books, 1990. Gems from a master storyteller.

Fuller, Buckminster. *Critical Path.* New York: St. Martin's Press, 1981. Includes Fuller's extraordinary personal credo.

Gallwey, W. Timothy. *The Inner Game of Tennis.* London: Jonathan Cape Ltd., 1975. Accessible, athletic Zen.

Gardner, Howard. *Frames of Mind: The Theory of Multiple Intelligences.* New York: Basic Books, Inc., 1983. Gardner posits seven distinct types of intelligence.

Gelb, Michael. *Body Learning: An Introduction to the Alexander Technique.* New York: Henry Holt & Company, 1987 (new edition, 1995). *Publishers Weekly* called this the most lucid book on the subject.

———. *Present Yourself! Captivate Your Audience With Great Presentations.* Rolling Estates, CA: Jalmar Press, 1988. An *Elements of Style* for public speakers.

———. *The NEW MIND MAP.* Washington, DC: High Performance Learning Center, 1991. (Illustrated by Nusa Gelb.) A road map for your mind.

Gelb, Michael, and Tony Buzan. *Lessons from the Art of Juggling: How to Achieve Your Full Potential in Business, Learning, and Life*. New York: Harmony Books, 1994. According to *Publishers Weekly*, "this uncommon approach to self-improvement has more to offer than other such guides and is a great deal more fun."

Gendlin, Eugene. *Focusing*. New York: Everst House, 1978. Harnessing the power of attention for personal growth.

Gibran, Kahil. *The Prophet*. London: Heinemann, 1926. "Pound for pound" it is one of the wisest, most profound guides to living ever written.

Gleick, James. *Genius: The Life and Science of Richard Feynman*. New York: Random House, 1992. A multidimensional portrait of the charismatic physicist.

Goldberg, Natalie. *Writing Down the Bones*. Boston: Shambhala Press, 1986. Goldberg masterfully leads her readers to greater self-expression, therapeutic catharsis, better writing and enlightenment.

Goodspeed, Bennett. *The Tao Jones Averages: A Guide to Whole Brained Investing*. New York: Penguin, 1983. Think synvergently and grow rich.

Gross, Ronald. *Peak Learning: A Master Course in Learning How to Learn*. Los Angeles: Jeremy P. Tarcher, Inc., 1991. An encyclopedia for continuous learning.

Hanks and Parry. *Wake Up Your Creative Genius*. Los Angeles: Crisp Publishers, 1991. A delightfully illustrated, playful guide to innovation.

Hart, Leslie. *How the Brain Works*. New York: Basic Books, 1975. Leslie Hart provides a fascinating look at the working of the human brain, emphasizing particularly its active, pattern-seeking nature.

Herrigel, Eugen. *Zen in the Art of Archery*. New York: Vintage Books edition, 1971. The original Zen application book, it offers penetrating insights into attaining excellence in any discipline.

Hirsh, Sandra, and Jean Kummerow. *Life Types*. New York: Warner Books, 1989. An introduction to the Myers-Briggs typology.

Hoffman, Edward. *The Right to Be Human: A Biography of Abraham Maslow*. Los Angeles: Jeremy P. Tarcher, Inc., 1988. A charming biography of the father of humanistic psychology and human-centered management.

Howard, Phillip. *The Death of Common Sense*. New York: Random House, 1994. Illuminates the effects of "left-brain psychosis" on our society.

Israel, Lana, and Buzan, Tony. *Brain Power for Kids*. Miami: BPK Publishers, 1989. Mind mapping for students.

Johnson, Barry. *Polarity Management: Identifying and Managing Unsolvable Problems*. Amherst, Mass.: HRD Press, 1992. Johnson's concept of polarity management is a brilliant example of synvergent thinking.

Kanter, Rosabeth. *When Giants Learn to Dance: Mastering the Challenge of Strategy, Management, and Careers in the 1990s.* New York: Simon & Schuster, Inc., 1989. Wisdom from the well-respected Harvard Business School professor.

Lao-tsu. *Tao Te Ching.* A New English Version with Forward and Notes by Stephen Mitchell. New York: Harper & Row, 1988. A masterpiece of synvergent thinking.

Luria, A. R. *The Man with a Shattered World.* Cambridge, Mass.: Harvard University Press, 1987. Startling insights into the mind and brain.

———. *The Mind of a Mnemonist.* Cambridge, Mass.: Harvard University Press, 1987. The fascinating study of a man who used synaesthesia to remember everything.

MacLean, Paul. *The Triune Brain in Evolution.* New York: Plenum, 1990.

Maslow, Abraham. *Toward a Psychology of Being,* 2nd ed. New York: Van Nostrand, 1968. The classic work of humanistic psychology.

May, Rollo. *The Courage to Create.* New York.: Bantam, 1976. A profound look at the creative process. May's work provided a major inspiration for the development of synvergent thinking.

McCormack, Mark. *What They Don't Teach You at Harvard Business School.* New York: Bantam Books, 1984.

Moore-Ede, Martin. *The Twenty-Four Hour Society.* New York: Addison-Wesley, 1993.

Ornstein, Robert. *The Evolution of Consciousness: The Origins of the Way We Think.* New York: Simon & Schuster, 1991. Ornstein charts the evolution of consciousness and the need for conscious evolution.

Peters, Tom, and Nancy Austin. *A Passion for Excellence.* New York: Warner Books, 1986. A valuable presentation of various corporate "models of excellence."

Restak, Richard M. *The Brain: The Last Frontier.* New York: Warner Books, 1979. A thorough, easy-to-read discussion of brain science.

Riso, Don Richard. *Personality Types: Using the Enneagram for Self-Discovery.* Boston: Houghton Mifflin Company, 1987. A ninefold typology based on ancient wisdom.

Roberts, Royston M. *Serendipity: Accidental Discoveries in Science.* New York: John Wiley & Sons, 1989.

Rossbach, Sarah. *Interior Design With Feng Shui.* New York: Dutton, 1987. A manual for creating brain-nourishing environments.

Rowan, Roy. *The Intuitive Manager.* New York: Berkley Books, 1986. An enjoyable overview based on the author's interviews with leaders in business, academia, and sports.

Rowse, A. L. *The Annotated Shakespeare.* New York: Greenwich House, Crown Books, 1984.

Russell, Peter. *The Brain Book.* London: Routledge & Kegan Paul, 1979. This superb text provides the research details behind Buzan's classic *Use Both Sides of Your Brain.*

————. *The White Hole in Time.* London: Routledge & Kegan Paul, 1992. A visionary's insightful prescriptions for our personal and planetary crises.

Samuels, M., and N. Samuels. *Seeing With the Mind's Eye.* New York: Random House, 1976. This comprehensive work provides fascinating information on the history and uses of visualization.

Saotome, Mitsugi. *Aikido and the Harmony of Nature.* Boston: Shambhala, 1993. Aikido springs from the synvergent transformation of violence into love.

Seligman, Martin. *Learned Optimism.* New York: Knopf, 1991. How to change your life by changing your mind.

Selye, Hans. *The Stress of Life.* New York: McGraw-Hill, 1978. The original work on stress that introduced the notion of "fight or flight."

Senge, Peter M. *The Fifth Discipline: The Art & Practice of the Learning Organization.* New York: Doubleday, 1990. How to see the forest.

Tannen, Deborah. *You Just Don't Understand.* New York: Ballantine Books, 1990. Why do many men avoid asking for directions? Why do many woman prefer to talk at breakfast rather than read the newspaper? This essential guide to intergender communication sheds light on these and many other mysteries.

Tarnas, Richard. *The Passion of the Western Mind: Understanding the Ideas That Have Shaped Our World.* New York: Ballantine Books, 1991. A masterpiece of compelling scholarship.

Toffler, Alvin. *Powershift.* New York: Bantam Books, 1990. How the knowledge revolution is reshaping the nature and distribution of power.

Turk, Christopher. *Effective Speaking: Communicating in Speech.* New York: E. & F. N. Spon, 1985. A very well-researched, detailed guide to presentation skills.

von Oech, Roger. *A Kick in the Seat of the Pants.* New York: Harper & Row, 1986.

————. *A Whack on the Side of the Head.* Revised edition. New York: Warner Books, 1990. Von Oech delivers what his titles promise.

Walton, Mary. *The Deming Management Method.* New York: Putnam, 1986.

Wenger, Win. *How to Increase Your Intelligence.* New York: Dell, 1975. I also recommend the numerous articles on creativity available through Wenger's Project Renaissance in Gaithersburg, Maryland.

Wheatley, Margaret. *Leadership and the New Science.* San Francisco: Berrett Koehler, 1992. "Old paradigm" organizations were based on a mechanistic, clockwork, Newtonian world view. The new paradigm springs from quantum, relativity, and chaos theory, fractals, dissipative structures, and strange attractors.

Wonder, Jacqueline. *Whole Brain Thinking.* New York: Ballantine Books, 1985. Test your brain dominance.

Zweig, Connie, and Jeremiah Abrams (eds). *Meeting the Shadow.* Los Angeles: Jeremy P. Tarcher, 1991. An enlightening walk through the dark side of the self.

About the High Performance
Learning Center® (HPL)

An international leadership training and consulting firm founded by Michael J. Gelb in 1982, HPL guides individuals and organizations to define and realize their highest aspirations. HPL helps leaders "walk their talk" to build teamwork, creativity, communication, trust, and organizational alignment. A catalyst for creative change, HPL bridges the gap between visions of exceptional quality, superior service, and personal fulfillment and everyday behavior. HPL's most popular programs and services (all customized to achieve specific client goals) include:

Mind Mapping® and Synvergent Thinking
Presentations as Leadership
Lessons from the Art of Juggling
Black Belt Business®
High Performance Sales
Leadership, Vision and Values
How to Think Like Leonardo da Vinci
The Executive Renaissance Seminar
One-on-One Executive Coaching with Michael J. Gelb
Visual Synthesis®—Simultaneous, artistic illustration of the content of meetings, conferences, and strategic planning sessions by Nusa Maal Gelb

Resources available from HPL include:
"Mind Mapping: How to Liberate Your Natural Genius" (four audiocassettes, produced by Nightingale-Conant)
"Mind Mapping and the Balanced Brain" (two audiocassettes with original "music for a brain-nourishing environment")
The New Mind Map (a road map to your mind)
and the following books:
•*Body Learning: An Introduction to the Alexander Technique (new edition)*
•*Present Yourself: Captivate Your Audience with Great Presentation Skills*
•*Lessons from the Art of Juggling: How to Achieve Your Full Potential in Business, Learning and Life (coauthor, Tony Buzan)*
•*The Mind Map Book: Radiant Thinking (by Tony Buzan)*

Contact:
Michael J. Gelb, President
High Performance Learning®
9844 Beach Mill Road
Great Falls, Virginia 22066
Telephone: (703) 757-7007, fax: (703) 757-7211
e-mail: gelb@hiperformlearning.com
website:http://www.hiperformlearning.com/gelb/

Besides the High Performance Learning Center, the sole source for *licensed* teachers of mind mapping is the Buzan Centers USA, Inc. founded by Tony Buzan and Vanda North.

Products available from the Buzan Centers include the million-plus seller *Use Both Sides of Your Brain, Lessons from the Art of Juggling, The Mind Map Book,* and *Buzan's Book of Genius.* Audiotapes include the new "Buzan on . . ." series and Michael Gelb's "Mind Mapping: How to Liberate Your Natural Genius." Other products include the new Charthouse video production, "If at first . . ." as well as mind map software and life management Systems. For more information on training courses, train-the-trainer programs or products, contact:
Buzan Centers Inc.
415 Federal Highway
Lake Park, Florida 33403
Telephone: (407) 881-0188 or fax: (407) 845-3210

INDEX

Michael J. Gelb is the originator of the concept of synvergent thinking and a pioneer in the development and teaching of mind mapping. Internationally acclaimed as an innovator in creativity, communication, and leadership training, Gelb has developed a unique, highly effective approach to his work as an organizational consultant and "Life Coach" for senior executives. His clients include AT&T, Du Pont, Amoco, Merck, Xerox, NPR, and the Liechtenstein Global Trading Co.